T0383860

REINVENTING
THE C-SUITE

There is a fundamental mismatch between the way we organise our senior management teams and the way modern commerce has evolved. Wrapping finesse, technology, rules, bureaucracy, and "science" around our C-Suite conventions, designed for nineteenth-century businesses, is not nearly enough to meet the challenges of modern business environments and practices.

This book is for executives who want to enable their C-Suite, and by extension their organizations, to survive and thrive into the future. It will help them to foresee future challenges and provide suggestions for new working practices at executive level to successfully adapt to those changes. How should executive teams organize themselves, reinvent their roles, and work with stakeholders to evolve and innovate? What is the role of the new C-grade executive – managers, leaders, or something else?

Executives and aspiring executives will find new challenges for organizations and ways to deal with them. Forward-thinking business students will find startling ideas and practical tools for viewing business and its activities. What is the next evolution of the executive function in organizations? This book explores how we can predict it, shape it, and succeed in it.

TERRY WHITE has been helping executives understand and drive positive change in their organizations for 30 years as an author, consultant, advisor, and mentor to C-level executives. He was a CIO for 10 years and has been advising executives on managing in the digital world for the past 20 years. He believes that today's executives are far too busy to be effective. He has helped executives reflect and think differently to lead their organizations to a new future.

REINVENTING THE C-SUITE

EVOLVING YOUR EXECUTIVE TEAM TO MEET TODAY'S CHALLENGES

Terry White

Routledge
Taylor & Francis Group

LONDON AND NEW YORK

First published 2020
by Routledge
2 Park Square, Milton Park, Abingdon, Oxon OX14 4RN

and by Routledge
52 Vanderbilt Avenue, New York, NY 10017

Routledge is an imprint of the Taylor & Francis Group, an
informa business

British Library Cataloguing-in-Publication Data
A catalogue record for this book is available from the
British Library

Library of Congress Cataloging-in-Publication Data
A catalog record has been requested for this book

ISBN: 978-0-367-34422-1 (hbk)
ISBN: 978-0-429-32692-9 (ebk)

Typeset in Minion
by Swales & Willis, Exeter, Devon, UK

CONTENTS

CONTENTS

PREFACE

L et's talk about revolution. Then let's talk about evolution.

There is a critical mismatch between the way we run our companies and the way modern commerce has evolved. Business cycles, complexity, speed, and rate of change are faster, more involved, more integrated and interactive, and more customer-driven than the way our organizations are structured and operate. We're still running our organizations as if it is 1950, albeit with more finesse, technology, rules, bureaucracy, and "science." However, you cannot compete with a motorcycle by pedaling your bicycle faster. And executives are pedaling as fast as they can. They will never catch up with the modern business motorcycle. And these are not only motorcycles, but they are also self-driving ones too. Executives in traditional C-Suites might be the best cyclists there are, but they're still cycling, while others are cruising, even flying.

> *The recent failure rate of chief executives in big American companies points in the same direction. A large proportion of CEOs of such companies appointed in the past ten years were fired as failures within a year or two ... This suggests that the jobs they took on had become undoable. The American record suggests not human failure but systems failure. Top management in big organizations needs a new concept.*[1]

These are the words of Peter Drucker, regarded as the founder of modern management, in his paper for *The Economist* in 2001. CEOs and executives are pedaling as fast as they can in an undoable job. We need a new revolutionary concept.

More than a century after the industrial revolution which birthed our corporations, and three industrial revolutions later, monolithic, slow, fiercely structured, and dominating organizations still, well … dominate. Dictatorships also dominate – by force, deception, and fear, much like many of our monolithic businesses. When 87% of the workforce is not engaged in their work, it's much like a dictatorship – keep your head down, do what you have to do, don't get noticed, and whatever you do, don't challenge the system. In the case of big business, like a dictatorship, the power is held by a few.

When I started this book, I had in mind to help executives realize the challenges facing them in general, and the digital challenge in particular. As I researched and explored the issues, I came to understand that digital is the lesser of the challenges executives face. The greatest challenge is the way they organize and run their operations, the way they control and manage, and that their priorities seem to be at odds with the primary purpose of business, shareholders, and employees. Technology merely accelerates the crisis. And crisis it is – corporate raiding of the economy, pillaging of resources, pollution of the environment, and control of employees' lives. This may seem a harsh indictment but read the papers and watch the news – it's very worrying. We need a revolution.

With the average C-Suite consisting of 50- 60-year olds, 70% male and white, one must also worry about the thinking and management styles they employ. As I say later in the book: "If a C-Suite is likened to a government, it would be a gerontocracy (run by elders), an androcracy (run by men) and an albocracy (run by white people). I'm not sure that's a recipe for success in this new world."

I've tried not to turn this into a polemic. Instead, I've tried to present the challenges in Part 1 and some potential solutions in Part 2. This book is for C-Suite executives who want to work less hard, think more, and create meaning in what they do. However, C-Suite executives are working at a frantic pace in an untenable job, so I doubt if they have time to read a book which may help them stop working so hard, and make their job do-able. So let's try a go-around – a Hail Mary pass if you will: This book is for shareholders who believe your organization should perform much better than it does, who want to help your executives focus on the right stuff, and who think that there must be another way of getting things done in the corporate world. Read the book, and if it makes sense to you, you have the power to apply pressure on the C-Suite for the changes that will not only improve the performance of the company in which you are a shareholder but also change the working lives of the C-Suite for the better. Another Hail Mary pass: This book is for farsighted managers and employees who want to work in a company that does the right things, performs more effectively, and values and allows you to think and fulfill your potential. This book is also for those people aspiring to get into the C-Suite. When you get there, and conditions haven't changed, it can only get worse. Business is getting more complex, faster, more integrated, and definitely more stressful. You're heading, as Peter Drucker says, into an undoable job. But when you get there, you will have the power to change the way the organization runs. Why not start now?

It's in the self-interest of C-Suite executives, shareholders, leading employees, and aspiring C-Suite members to read this book. I hope you do read it, and that it is a game-changer for you.

Let me finish with the words of A.A Milne[2]: He wrote a poem about Edward Bear (Winnie-the-Pooh) being dragged down the stairs behind Christopher Robin. Pooh's head kept bumping down each step, and he wondered if there was a better way of coming downstairs, "... *if only he could stop bumping for a moment and think of it ...*"

There is a better way, of course. But our executives are too busy to stop bumping for a moment and think of it. Now's the time to stop bumping.

NOTES

1 Peter Drucker, "Will Corporations Survive?" *The Economist*, November 3, 2001.
2 A.A. Milne, *Winnie the Pooh,* Dutton Children's Books, 2006.

CHAPTER ONE

What is management and how did it get to where it is today?

L et's talk about revolution, then let's talk about power.

REVOLUTIONS AND THE START OF MANAGEMENT

R evolutions can be political, economic, cultural, religious, and
intellectual. Either way, revolutions seek a fundamental change –
usually to power and organization. Some revolutions result in relatively
sudden change, and some take generations to take effect. Probably the
first revolution was Agricultural, which took place 10,000 years ago with
the shift from hunter-gatherer societies to a society based on stationary
farming. Usually, revolutions affect more than the immediate subject of
the revolution – the agricultural revolution transformed agriculture yes,
but also changed society, health, the environment, religion, politics, and
eventually numbers and accounting. Yet, there are still some hunter-
gatherers after all these years.

The story of management starts with the industrial revolution. Before the
industrial revolution, there were few organizations – the church, the military,
and a few trading, agricultural, and construction organizations – but no
recognizable "management." Back then managers were called agents or factors.

The industrial revolution started in about 1760, with a transition from hand
production methods to machines, and new chemical manufacturing and
iron production processes. The era of mass production had arrived. It was
a turning point in history, affecting income growth, population settlement,
urbanization, society, work, culture, the environment, and even religion.
Interestingly, it changed thinking from "stability is good" to "growth is
good" – and as we'll see, growth is not the panacea it's made out to be.

With mass production, labor in workshops and factories needed to be
supervised, and business owners appointed people to manage their factories
for them. The management undertaking concerned itself with the execution
of production at scale. Managers were tasked with planning the work

and workflow, employing specialized people where needed, monitoring production (with some basic accounting thrown in), monitoring and controlling the quality of goods produced, and reporting to the owner on production outputs. They certainly weren't concerned with the outcomes of their production which resulted in poor working conditions, overcrowding in cities, depopulation of rural areas, chemical pollution, cholera outbreaks, air and water pollution, and smog which caused lung disease. There were positive outcomes such as a decrease in prices, general availability of goods, and the eventual improvement in standards of living.

Management was a revolution within the industrial revolution. Managers supervised production lines but produced nothing themselves. This was seen as the efficient application of Adam Smith's concept of the division of labor. Speaking of concepts, yet another revolution within the management revolution was taking place. As the industrial revolution proceeded, business "scholars" began to study how people and processes worked and could work more efficiently. They tested concepts and developed theories about efficiency, production quality and consistency, and predictability of production to optimize outputs. As the knowledge base grew and "scientific" business theories were postulated and tested, it became possible for these scholars to teach others, and in 1881, the first higher institutions of learning about management started with the Wharton School. Joseph Wharton was a wealthy industrialist, lobbyist, and scientist. He had apprenticed as an accountant, as an apprenticeship was the only way of gaining business knowledge at the time, and he conceived of a school that would teach business and economic principles and practices. He donated $100,000 for the establishment of the school at the University of Pennsylvania, and they introduced and extended his curriculum. Other universities soon followed. The profession and discipline of management was born. Apprenticeships were reserved for trade professions, and management became a social class.

Management activities and their focus evolved over time. Rita Gunther McGrath, a professor at Columbia Business School and one of the top management thinkers today, suggests that management has gone through three eras with each era emphasizing a different theme:[1] execution, expertise, and empathy. The industrial revolution management era was focused on the performance of production. With the introduction of business schools and the professionalization of management, people were hired into management because of their expertise – in the management discipline. The execution era was concerned with creating scale and efficiency, while the expertise era is concerned with creating advanced services. Finally, McGrath suggests that we are entering a period where organizations need to create customer experiences. For this, managers need to empathize with customers and staff to create good experiences. That we have entered a new era of management is beyond doubt, but I believe it is more nuanced than clearly differentiated eras: Some managers will still focus on execution, scaling, and efficiency, and others will create new and advanced services. However, I believe senior executives will need to focus on very different things, and this is what the book is about.

However, before we rush into what executives should be doing, let's look at two types of executive and power.

POWER IN ORGANIZATIONS AND MANAGEMENT'S POWER

So far, I've used "management" as a universal term to describe those who direct organizations, and that's probably true. However, there are two types of people who run organizations, those who choose the organization's direction and goals, and those who direct activities to achieve those goals. The first are leaders and the second are managers. Together, let's call them executives – people fulfill a role to achieve an end. There are distinct differences between managers and leaders: Managers design and control the organizational "machine," while leaders deal with people, vision, and concepts. There are refinements to this generalization – most managers deal with people of course, but how they deal with them is different. Many leaders manage and many managers lead, but for clarity let's keep the distinction separate. Both leaders and managers "make things happen," but generally leaders work on what is to happen and managers work on how it is to happen. Management is mostly an engineering discipline, while leadership is a social discipline. Moreover, the power that managers and leaders use is mainly different. We need to look at power in organizations to understand this better.

Organizational power is the capability to accomplish things through other people. Power is many things, but this definition is useful for us. It ascribes neither positive or negative meaning to power – it's the use of power by individuals that makes it positive or negative. There are many types of organizational power, but seven serve our purpose:

- Legitimate power is the power conferred by the organizational hierarchy. A CEO should have more power than most, but sometimes others have more power because they possess other forms of power. Legitimate power is also called titular power; the power ascribed to a title.
- Consequence power that comes from being able to engender consequences. These can be both positive and negative. The power to reward is a consequence of power usually enabled by the legitimate power of the individual. Similarly, the power to enforce adverse outcomes, for instance, to initiate disciplinary measures, is also a consequence power. Some consequence power can be subtle – making resources unavailable, or indeed yourself unavailable, is a form of negative power, while the authority to assign interesting projects or promote people is positive.
- Referent power is usually based on who you can refer issues to. Furthermore, their power is referred back to you. A CEO's assistant has loads of referent power, because even though he doesn't refer issues to the CEO, the fact that he can do so, confers power on the assistant.
- Connection power comes from who you know. You can get things done through other people. For example, a salesperson might know a friend of a CEO to whom she wants to pitch. She uses her connection to get an appointment with the CEO.

- Informational power comes from what you know. I once ran a strategy workshop for a division of a company. On the final day, the CEO was invited to review the strategy. The CEO listened politely then, bless him, said: "You don't know this, but your entire division is being split up into other units. However, it's still a nice strategy." This is the worst use of informational power. Positive forms of informational power come to people who are up to date on the latest developments, regulations, and policies.
- Expert power comes from your expertise. Some engineers and contractors can hold the organization to ransom because of their expert power. A more positive form is when people know to approach you because your expertise is valuable and often resolves a tricky problem.
- Charismatic power is power conferred on you because people like you, or they are drawn to you. Sometimes this is also a form of moral power, where people are attracted to what you stand for.

Leaders and managers have both types of power but in different proportions. A leader can be a manager and vice versa, but because their roles are different, they should focus on their specialty. Furthermore, they need each other. An example of managers working with leaders is the unlikely pairing of Winston Churchill and Clement Attlee. Churchill was a profoundly conservative politician (he was against universal suffrage for instance), and Attlee was the leader of the Labor Party. In 1940, Churchill became Prime Minister to lead the British war effort, and in 1942, Attlee became Deputy Prime Minister. Churchill was an orator, visionary and strategist, while Attlee was an implementor and enabler. They needed each other. When asked what Churchill had done to help win the war, Attlee said: "He talked about it."

Leaders have legitimate power conferred on them by the people who follow them. They always have charismatic power, and often have informational and expert power. Managers have legitimate and consequence power. One of the primary power sources that managers also have is informational power, but we will see that the digital revolution is undercutting this power. They may also use their referent power.

Unfortunately, managers are often promoted into leadership positions and find themselves unable to perform, because they do not have power conferred on them by their people, nor do they have the charismatic power to attract people to themselves.

The summary of the two types of executives can be neatly summed up as follows: Leaders are about effectiveness – knowing what to do and having people willingly to do it. Managers are about efficiency – ensuring that what is done is done well.

THE IMPLICATIONS OF THE EVOLUTION OF MANAGEMENT

Now let's talk about the implications of the evolution of management: I've mentioned revolution, fundamental change, power and organization, effects beyond the immediate revolution, and touched on the fact that in spite of the revolution, some people still live in a pre-revolutionary world. I've talked about the evolution of management and the management class. Finally, I observed in passing that "growth" became the new ideal and objective for organizations and suggested that growth may not be all it's made out to be.

Let's look at each of these and the effects and implications that live below the surface.

Most revolutions are peaceful affairs, except regime change. However, there is one element common to all revolutions – those people that benefitted from the previous conditions resist the change. In political revolutions, this resistance is usually by force and repression. In corporations, the opposition is subtler but no less effective. John Hagel[2] talks of an organization's immune system and antibodies that act to destroy any threat to the status quo. There is a significant revolution in business today – we're in the third industrial revolution (the digital revolution) heading into the fourth (essentially the fusing of the physical, digital, and biological worlds). And organizational antibodies are working overtime, much of it coming from the management class. Organizational antibodies will agree readily and vigorously with an advocate of change, then just as readily and vigorously undermine the advocate and sabotage the change. Another thing about revolutions – those resisting the change believe themselves to be right and righteous as will many managers who read this book and disagree with its message.

Revolutions are about fundamental change. The foundations of a system are rocked and even destroyed. In the third industrial revolution, the economy and commercial system are being shaken at its foundations. We have to rethink how organizations work, what they are for, who the organization is, who works in organizations, and how we manage performance and rewards. We need to look at the boundaries of our organizations and why organizations even exist. We need to examine the education system that feeds our organizations and consider if it is providing fit-for-purpose employees. We must urgently reconsider the beliefs that drive the actions of organizations and reexamine the functions within organizations. Finally, and importantly, we need to look at the roles and purpose of the people charged with leading and managing our organizations. If we are to cope with the changes brought about by the third industrial revolution, and ready ourselves for the fourth industrial revolution, every foundational belief, structure, system, and process is on the examination table.

Revolutions affect power and structure. We will see that most of the managerial class in our organizations is about power and structure. And the ego. They will defend their status vigorously. A little more management history: During the industrial revolution, managerial positions corresponded with the manufacturing or assembly route. The change to structured organizational hierarchies had its roots in the military. As organizations grew more substantial, the managerial positions became further removed from the organization's core activities, and increasingly geared toward delivering commands from higher-ups and exerting control on others who occupied subordinate roles.[3] As managers became more removed from operational activities, they came to rely on legitimate, consequence, and informational power to get their job done. In the third industrial revolution, digitization undercuts hierarchies, and freely available information undermines power positions. Moreover, if revolutions affect power and structures, then the manager – who draws his authority from the bureaucracy and his power from the organization and information – is the most likely to resist.

Revolutions have effects beyond their immediate sphere of influence. For instance, the French Revolution ushered in new land ownership rules, resulted in a declining birthrate, promoted small-scale entrepreneurship, formalized the adoption of the metric system, and through the Jacobins, initiated communist thought. The third industrial revolution has changed society and how we interact with each other. It has improved our access to information and how we are educated. It has transformed medicine, science, manufacturing, and business. It has changed how and where we work. It has transformed the book distribution and publishing industries. How and where we travel has also changed. And for small businesses and large it has allowed us to achieve scale without mass.[4] It has even changed how I researched this book, who I talked to, how I checked my facts, and how it was published.

The digital revolution hasn't changed managers much. Which segues nicely into the next point: In spite of the revolution, some people still live in a pre-revolutionary world. Yes, managers use the technology, work in much the same way as the rest of us, and access the same information as we do. *Financial Times* journalist Simon Caulkin examined management practices today[5] and said: "Managers are still building mass-production organizations fit for the early twentieth century, based on hierarchy, standardization, and compliance, rather than flexible, human-centered outfits in which technology is not a threat but a partner of both employees and customers." Managers still manage performance the way they've always done and plan and execute initiatives in the same way. They even monitor and control in the same way and report the same things.

Most importantly, they again measure the same things – they still subscribe to the McNamara Fallacy. Robert McNamara was the US Secretary of Defense during the Vietnam War, and he expressed a view of measurement which goes like this: Step 1 – Measure whatever can easily be measured. Step 2 – Disregard that which can't be easily measured. Step 3 – Presume that what can't be measured easily is unimportant. Step 4 – Believe that what can't be measured easily doesn't exist. This is madness, but how many of our managers don't measure well-being, aspirations, health, work/life balance, the effect of their organization's products and services, the effect of open-plan offices on productivity, and the effect of what they say? How many believe that human resources are, well resources, to be used as and when needed and that the measure of a person is as a cost, not an asset that adds value? None of these are easy to measure, but with the digital revolution, they are much easier than they were. Charles Handy, whom we will hear much more from, added a step to the McNamara Fallacy[6]: Step 2 – Assume that what we can measure leads to the desired outcome. The management belief that if it can't be measured, it can't be managed is bunkum. The world is much more complicated than our measures of it. Look at the Reinventing the C-Suite website blog (www.terrygrey.com) for some examples of and discussion on the McNamara fallacy.

MANAGEMENT AS A PROFESSION AND CLASS

Management as a profession and discipline has evolved and continues to evolve. But some managers not so much. Most managers believe that management involves planning, organizing, directing, and controlling. Some definitions add that management is about working with human, financial, and physical resources to achieve organizational objectives. All good so far. However, I believe these functions are a small part of modern management in a digital world, and even then, the activities that are needed to carry out these functions are fundamentally changed by the digital revolution. Forward-thinking management is surely about engaging people – a 2016 Gallup poll showed that only 13% of employees are engaged at work[7] – ensuring their effectiveness, and helping them deliver rather than driving them to perform. New managerial work is people work, not systems and process work. Finally, and most critically, a manager should constantly learn and apply that learning. The word "evolve" has three meanings: to develop new characteristics in response to the environment; to gain through experience; and to work something out – as in "to evolve a theory." Modern managers should be doing all of these.

Managers as a class became prominent when they removed themselves from the shop floor. They have become further removed over time and usually see themselves as interventionists when things go wrong and controllers and orchestrators at other times. Planners yes, but ultimately they will direct the implementation of their plan. Most large businesses appear to be like the centrally planned regimes of the old communist world. Control is everything, and people are regarded as units of production. They are not a company at all – if "company" means companions and community. In a community, people have an interest in the outputs of that community. They are citizens rather than human resources, and they hold their leaders accountable for results. They do have responsibilities, but they also have rights that go beyond the standard workplace rights given by management. Community rights extend to what the community exists for, what it produces, how it is built, and who has legitimate power in the community. But companies mostly don't work that way, and they may see the same fate as the Soviet Union, with open revolt and eventual dissolution, or as the ruling class in the French Revolution. Management as a class has an allure for managers, but the class is exposed when there is easy access to information when communication is instant and widespread, and when hierarchies and control can be bypassed – all of which are possible after the digital revolution.

GROWTH

Growth is good. It raises the standard of living. But here we come up against the McNamara fallacy: Standard of living is measured as GDP per capita. There is no indication that the lives of people are better. Indeed the average person is healthier, wealthier, and lives longer and better than before. But are they happier, more fulfilled, less stressed, more family-oriented, or do they have more leisure time?

Growth creates choices. Imagine a world where there is no growth. This means that the pie size remains the same, and everyone must compete for a piece of that pie. Those who cannot compete could become moribund and depressed. They could also become envious of those who do have their slice of the pie. Social unrest could follow.

Growth should at least keep pace with population increase – if growth is less than the population increase the measure of standard of living goes down. However, growth certainly has not delivered on the promise of prosperity for all. An Oxfam report[8] in 2016 showed that just 62 individuals had the same wealth as 3.6 billion people – the poor half of the world. It gets worse: 99% of the world's population owned 55% of the global wealth in 2010, while 1% owned 44%. After five years, that same 99% of the population owned less than 50%, and the 1% owned more than they did. Growth that creates wealth for 1% of the population, but which decreases the wealth of the overwhelming majority is a dangerous thing. (Spreading the wealth of the 1% around won't make much of a difference to the 99%. But ensuring that further growth is directed at the 99% and not the 1% might make a substantial difference.) Growth that trashes the environment and steals its resources impoverishes the future at the expense of the present and is immoral as well as being shortsighted. Growth that replaces people with technology, with no alternatives for those replaced is a dangerous path to revolution. Growth that measures success only by what we can measure and ignores what we can't measure is just plain stupid.

We need managers, executives, and leaders. However, we need them to realize that the world has changed, that we have changed, and that they must change. We need leaders and managers to help us into the future, for surely no-one else will.

THE TYPICAL C-SUITE

There are many generalizations in the book, both in the use of terms (like "management" and "C-Suite") and in the assumption that all executives and their teams are the same. They're not and shouldn't be. But the facts are worrying. Of the Fortune 500 companies, 70% of the executive and 95% of CEOs are white and male, so "he" is not a generalization, nor is it sexist. But it is worrying. Where are the radicals, the activists, the youth, the racially diverse opinions, and where are the women?

Let's also generalize age: In America and Europe, the average age of executives in the C-Suite is 54, with a tenure of 5.3 years. Let's think about that for a moment. When current C-Suite members entered the workforce, the internet didn't exist, cell-phones didn't exist, social media didn't exist, and computer systems were solely concerned with finance. I know because I was there: I was a Facilities Manager in an IT installation.

But here's the thing. If a C-Suite is likened to a government, it would be a gerontocracy (run by elders), an androcracy (run by men), and an albocracy (run by white people). I'm not sure that's a recipe for success in this new world.

The average life of a corporation has dropped from 60 years in the 1950s, to under 20 years right now. Some research indicates a 14-year lifespan for companies. So the average tenure of the C-Suite is between one third and one quarter of the expected life of their company. That's not a very long time to make a difference. So the actions that they take should be meaningful and useful. This is why, perhaps, I may be strident or even polemic, because we're all holding our breath.

NOTES

1 Rita Gunther McGrath, Management's Three Eras: A Brief History, *Harvard Business Review*, 2014. https://hbr.org/2014/07/managements-three-eras-a-brief-history, [Accessed March 2019].
2 John Hagel, *Scaling Edges: How to Radically Transform Your Organization*, Idea Bite Press, 2014.
3 Bonnitta Roy, *A Brief History of Management, Medium – Our Future at Work*, 2016. https://medium.com/open-participatory-organized/a-brief-history-of-management-23361290a08b, [Accessed March 2019].
4 Erik Brynjolfsson, Andrew McAfee, Michael Sorell and Feng Zhu, Scale without Mass: Business Process Replication and Industry Dynamics, *Harvard Business School Working Knowledge*, 2006. https://hbswk.hbs.edu/item/scale-without-mass-business-process-replication-and-industry-dynamics, [Accessed March 2019].
5 Simon Caulkin, Era of Management-led Growth Held Hostage by Old Ideas that Refuse to Die, *Financial Times*, 2014. www.ft.com/content/cc4a40c4-085a-11e4-9afc-00144feab7de, [Accessed March 2019].
6 Charles Handy, *The Second Curve: Thoughts on Reinventing Society*, Random House Books, 2016.
7 Steve Crabtree, Worldwide, 13% of Employees are Engaged at Work, *Gallup*, 2016. https://news.gallup.com/poll/165269/worldwide-employees-engaged-work.aspx, [Accessed March 2019].
8 Oxfam An Economy for the 1%, *210 Oxfam Briefing Paper*, 2016. www.oxfam.org/en/research/economy-1, [Accessed November 2019].

PART 1

The challenges facing the C-Suite

This book is divided into two sections: The first one examines the challenges facing C-Suite executives, and the second part offers suggestions on how the C-Suite should respond to these and other challenges.

The structure of Part 1 is organized as a simple process flow diagram – examining the inputs (what executives get to work with), operations (how organizations work today), and outputs (what customers expect) – as shown in Figure 2.1:

Inputs	Operations	Outputs
Education input to the C-Suite Generations in the workplace Information as a challenge	The world of work Digital transformation in organizations Functions and processes Change, pressure and speed	What customers want yesterday Business ecosystems

Figure 2.1 The structure of Part 1

Each of the elements in the diagram is a chapter, so let's get started.

CHAPTER TWO

The educational system
product and its inputs
to organizations

John Hagel[1] says that technology increases competitive pressure, speeds up change, amplifies impacts (a small start-up in China can change an industry worldwide), and connects everyone. So how do organizations compete when a developing country can make products better, faster, and cheaper than developed countries? How do we compete when the product we produce today can be obsolete tomorrow? Moreover, how do we compete when ideas are accessible worldwide – there's no monopoly on the new? The only answer is learning and innovation. And this is where our schooling systems are failing us and the organizations that depend on the product of schooling.

INDUSTRIAL STRENGTH SCHOOLING

Have a look at a TED talk by Sir Ken Robinson on his take on our schooling system. (Just search for "Ken Robinson Education.") He says that most schooling systems are trying to reinvent themselves to answer two questions: How do we educate our children to take their place in the economy given the rapid changes in the economy? And, how do we preserve our cultural identity in a globalized world? The problem, says Robinson, is that we are trying to answer these questions by looking backward. His thesis is that our current schooling system is designed for the first industrial revolution, and with an either-or mentality – either you're clever or you're not. The backward-looking view of "clever" is that clever people are academic – they are capable of deductive reasoning, and they have good reading, writing, and arithmetic skills. This mentality excludes most of the kids in modern society, and labels them as "stupid" – but as you will see they are not.

In 1968, Professor George Land and Beth Jarman conducted a test on 1,600 children aged 4–5 to test their creativity. Ninety-eight percent of the children tested out at a creative genius level. This surprised them, so they conducted the test on the same kids when they were ten years old, and only 30% were tested as creative. So they did the test again when they were 15 years old, and the result was 12%. They stopped the program at this time, but they did test an adult population of an average age of 31, and the result was 2%. The results are clear: Creativity diminishes as we get older. Or is that true? Land and Robinson both believe that creativity remains innate in people. We have it schooled out of us.

To understand this, consider what Land calls divergent and convergent thinking. Divergent thinking is creative, produces multiple solutions for any one problem, and visualizes many possibilities. Convergent thinking is critical, judgmental, testing and deciding. Both are necessary, but the schooling system forces us to have the convergent thinking mode switched on all the time. So when we think of an idea, we simultaneously judge it. Schooling puts a positive spin on this by saying we should think of an idea and test whether it is right. What they don't accept is multiple answers to a problem, nor do they give children time to expand on possibilities. School tests look for the one right answer. George Land shows that fear chases divergent thinking right out of the brain. So exams, with the stress that they induce, cannot expect creativity. In short, convergent thinking asks: "Is it right?," while divergent thinking asks: "What is possible?"

There is a difference between schooling and education. As Mark Twain said: "I never let school get in the way of my education." Many scholars need to bypass the schooling system to get their education. I used to bunk school to go and read. Textbooks, novels, and science magazines – that's where I got my education. Indeed "school" has two meanings – it means the institution set up to educate, but it also means to discipline and train. It seems that the latter sense has taken hold – this definition is of course usually applied to horses.

The majority of our schools are designed to produce standardized individuals who can read, write, and do some arithmetic. Their message is clear: Conform, work hard, do well, go to college, get a job. But the schooling system is only a recent phenomenon. Before the industrial revolution, limited schooling was available to the rich. Primarily, education was provided by apprenticeships. With the advent of factories, we needed to set up factories for humans – schools – to manufacture people to work in our factories. And our schools are designed as factories, not for education.

If a kid is inattentive, distracted, asks too many questions, or even questions the schooling itself, they are often drugged into compliance. Children are bombarded with stimuli and information by TV, games, and social media, yet are expected to sit through a dull lesson in which they have no interest. Aesthetic interest is visual, experience-based, here-and-now, curious, and creative. In school, this behavior is often deemed disruptive at worst, and non-conformist at best. We give anesthetics to aesthetics with amphetamines and methylphenidate.

Children are produced in batches (much like a factory), in classes based on the year the kids enter the system. It's as if schools stamp our kids with a date of manufacture. Indeed, the "Class of '84" is an echo of the batch process.

While our children are in class, they are alone. They are tested individually when it is clear that working in groups is more productive and that learning is often better. In business, teams work together to complete work. Because the schooling system hasn't found a creative way of testing groups without averaging the individuals, standardized, single student testing continues.

School marginalizes people. Firstly, if you are brighter or "slower" than your age group, you're in trouble. Gifted or "dull" kids are treated the same or are placed in gifted or "dull" classes. The schooling system is set up to make teaching more comfortable, not to make learning easier or appropriate to the learner. There's very little in the school system that's about the individual. Some people learn well in groups, others as individuals, some learn visually or orally, others learn by reading. Some learn well in the morning, others in the evening. Some are artistic and creative; others are logical and deductive.

School is a bell-ridden system, regulating the lives of scholars in preparation for factory work. The modern workplace has no bells or sirens, indeed often has no prescribed work hours. Indeed, there is sometimes no set workplace, yet school puts kids in classes. It's as if they're saying: "This is where you learn and work." But learning happens everywhere.

Children sit at desks to prepare them for workstation work – processing portions of work serially. Teaching is also organized in timed batches – called "periods" – and the teacher goes through a set syllabus for every year. The knowledge that kids gain in school is often inappropriate to work-life, and certainly has an expiry date.

Schools teach from prescribed textbooks (and some internet access) which are, well, prescribed. These are set down as part of the curriculum and offer a sanitized and generic view of the world. At university, I had a lecturer who used one textbook word for word, yet prescribed two others. I found his textbook and stopped attending his lectures. Learners are smarter than the education system gives them credit for. They can think, but the prescribed curriculum sets them on a path that is easiest for the teacher to navigate.

Schools grade students as if good grades are the goal. The goal is education and grades merely show how well a student tests. Schools have standardized testing, a form of testing that requires all students to answer the same question or select from a common bank of questions. Standardized testing scores the result in a standardized manner and normalizes the result. This produces a relative score (better or worse than other test-takers) rather than an absolute score. Schools do not monitor learner success or failure once they are out of the school system. They do not test fit-for-purpose graduates. They do not ask their students about their well-being or their satisfaction with their schooling.

Schools cater for only two of the eight or nine intelligences that children bring to class. In 1983, Howard Gardner of Harvard University defined, among other things, spatial, intrapersonal, and interpersonal intelligence. Formal schooling only tends to address two of Gardner's intelligences: Linguistic and logical-mathematical intelligence. Businesses certainly need these two types (otherwise the schooling system would have been restructured years ago), but they also need spatial, intrapersonal, and interpersonal intelligence among others. Gardner didn't mention creative intelligence, but that is one of the critical needs in business and governments, and especially in small businesses. Spatial intelligence is the ability to visualize things, and the ability to see things as models of reality. (There are other factors in the intelligences we are looking at, but I'm focusing on those most useful to businesses, large and small.) Intrapersonal intelligence is the ability to understand oneself, which we will see is one of the significant elements of executive success. Interpersonal intelligence is the capacity to understand others and to work with others and get them to work with you. There's probably a "complexity" intelligence – the ability to synthesize complex issues and navigate in a complex environment. Research has shown that dealing with complexity is one of the critical skills that executives need when they move from management to the C-Suite. Spatial intelligence may go some way towards dealing with complexity.

School is mandatory. While all children need an education, is the schooling system the only way to get it? If school were optional, what would the other options be? Remember that education is needed to achieve an outcome. The outcome of school is a certificate which could get you a job or a place at university. The result is not necessarily educated people, creative people or fit-for-employment people. Globally the youth unemployment rate is 13.1%, with developed countries at 14.3% and developing countries at 9.4%. Where economies are growing, there are more jobs. For more than 10% of aspiring work seekers, the message is: "Don't look for a job, create your own." The mandatory school experience does little to prepare them for this, and a certificate is useless to them. In business, a 10% non-standard product would be a disaster. There need to be more options than school.

In the third industrial revolution, and heading into the fourth, our schooling system has not kept up – either in the way it teaches or in the "product" that it produces.

Certainly, syllabi have changed to include economics and finance, as well as computer coding, but again these are behind the times. For instance, a university professor told me that there is very little need for coding in the business environment. New techniques called "no-code/low-code" are gaining ground. The technology is available to code automatically provided you map out what you want and what you want to achieve – a spatial intelligence, while coding is a logical intelligence. Financial courses tend to focus on accounting, which is not a bad thing, but we need entrepreneurs, whose finances focus on cashflow, simple budgeting, loan agreements, and banking. The US Census Bureau found that 64% of new employment is provided by small businesses and that they represent about 50% of the private-sector payroll, so entrepreneurs need some payroll and tax skills.

But we're getting off the point. Charles Handy[2] has been looking at the education system since the 1980s. Here are some of his thoughts about education:

- Learning to think and do is as important as learning facts and figures.
- Teachers usually learn more than their pupils.
- Curiosity is more important than discipline.
- No-one is stupid; they are merely not curious or interested.
- Three or four heads are better than one in most situations.
- Most learning happens outside the classroom.
- Examinations test only the absorption of knowledge shortly after its reception.

He makes many other points: for instance, why is education structured as a set of hoops to jump through, rather than a journey structured for individuals? And that school needs to imitate work and life beyond its boundaries.

Here are some questions we should ask:

- Why do schools test individuals rather than teams? (Ken Robinson says that at work it's called collaboration and teamwork; at school, it's called cheating.)
- Why do teachers teach, rather than setting teaching goals for students to show each other?
- How are gifted or "dull" students accommodated in formal schooling? (I was a dull scholar.)
- Why are some kids labeled stupid or sub-grade at school, when after they leave school they thrive?
- Why is a student grouped by age, or even grouped at all?
- Why is school so different from life and work?

Let's also look at the product that schools produce. Reading, writing, arithmetically-sound school leavers enter a world where creativity, initiative, a learning mindset, and collaboration are valued skills. And that's just the school system's "good" performers. What about the "could do better," "is lazy," does not concentrate" school leavers? (These comments were made about me, and I went on to graduate cum laude with a master's in commerce.) I only came into my own once formal education and examinations were over. My honors year was mostly project work, and my master's was about thinking and research. The problem is intelligence and how formal schooling only addresses a portion of the intelligences that scholars bring with them to school.

THE CHALLENGE OF OUR EDUCATIONAL SYSTEM

The challenges facing the C-Suite is that they are products of the schooling system and that the people who are entering their organizations are the same standardized product.

We need a revolution in schooling – the first and last school revolution was about creating factories for humans to populate our factories. The third and fourth industrial revolutions need a second educational revolution. Because we can't see the fifth industrial revolution, it means that we can prepare for the present, but there's no reason educators cannot look beyond the fourth industrial revolution.

The third industrial revolution is characterized by connectivity and mature computing power. It is a digital, networked, globalized business environment. Design and manufacturing are computerized. Products are smart and personalized. Marketing and customer feedback are digitalized and near real-time. Computing power allows organizations to achieve "scale without mass"[3] where they can replicate themselves without investing in the infrastructure needed in traditional "bricks and mortar" enterprises. Organizations cannot run without sophisticated computer systems that speed up, standardize, monitor, and drive business processes. Knowledge-work is dominant. Artificial intelligence and big data inform decisions. Business networks and ecosystems supply customer needs. People work from home, or on the train, or from coffee shops. Work hours are flexible. Information flows freely and is available to the lowliest of worker. In short, networking and computers have created a Schumpeterian economy – where old businesses are destroyed and replaced with new ones. The lifespan of businesses has dropped from 60 years to under 20 years. Disruption, churn, and transformation are all continuous rather than discrete events.

The fourth industrial revolution is still in its infancy, but it is characterized by the blurring of the lines between the physical, digital, and biological systems. While it is yet to play out, it includes biotechnology, robotics, nano-technology, decentralized consensus, and additive manufacturing.

The implications of the third and fourth industrial revolutions for schooling are that education can be distributed, networked, parallel, available anywhere, personalized, test free, intelligence-targeted, modular, age-independent, fast or slow, and is easily replicated. Perhaps with the fourth industrial revolution, education can be worn, delivered by robots, consensus-driven, self-moderated, and optional. Look at the website "Reinventing the C-Suite" for a blog post on my take on what twenty-first century schooling might be.

The current schooling system is a challenge for executives, yes, but it is only a challenge and not a roadblock. Apart from lobbying for a change in the schooling system, (should businesses set up their own schools?) executives can do a lot to meet these challenges. Of course, they need to start with themselves. How can they free the creative genius that was locked away by their schooling? They can practice divergent thinking – generating possibilities and ideas without engaging any form of convergent thinking. They need to look at their intelligences. There is no doubt that modern executives are smart, but success in the C-Suite depends on intrapersonal and interpersonal intelligence. The other intelligence they need to develop if they don't have it is the ability to deal with complexity.

The challenge of staff educated in the formal schooling system is the same. It's not an accident that organizations are starting to see culture and capability as more critical to success than organizing people, processes, and technologies. Executives can work on a culture where creativity is welcomed and encouraged. A formal innovation program won't cut it – it's formal and it's a program. Creativity is neither of those. Encourage divergent thinking – let people come to you with possibilities, not solutions. Solutions are easy because we've been schooled to them, possibility thinking is difficult because it has been schooled out of us.

There is more for executives to do when looking at the schooling system. Don't look back to solve problems – what's worked before may not work in the future. Look at your organization for the first industrial revolution features. Where in the business do you run things like a factory where this is not necessary or even detrimental? Look at your smart and "stupid" people. Clever people should be unleashed, "stupid" people are probably required to operate using intelligences they don't have while ignoring intelligences that they do have. Disruptive people are usually disengaged, are not interested, and use their creativity for the wrong ends. A clear vision of the future will allow disruptive people to create "outside" possibilities. Think about intelligence when assembling teams – complimentary intelligences can achieve more than similar intelligences in a group.

Look at fear in the organization – it banishes creativity and innovation. Uncertainty is everywhere and it should be harnessed through divergent thought. The phenomenon of managing through fear is common and fear-inducing managers should be identified and coached out of this practice. Usually, managers who use fear as a tool are fearful themselves. Look at your performance reviews – they induce fear and the purpose of them may not be in the individuals' interests.

Think about education in the organization. Not training. Remember that education comes from everywhere and from anywhere. For example, send your financial people out to the branches, or to customers – they'll learn a lot. Allow staff to teach; that's how they learn. Ecosystem thinking can be applied to learning. With modern technology, what I'll call "centers of thinking excellence" are easy to set up. For example, you could set up a center of thinking excellence around the customer experience. Anyone, including customers, can join. Counter staff, secretaries, finance clerks, and drivers can all provide insights into how the customer experiences your business. And they can all provide divergent thinking that differs from the managers and marketing people whose formal job it is to think about these things.

Look at how jobs are structured. Charles Handy talks of the "empty donut" job where 30% of the work is prescribed and 70% is created by the individual. This gives people options and allows them to create their own jobs, and it also motivates them and often throws up hidden surprises for the organization. This may seem a recipe for chaos, and it could be, but a little divergent thinking by you and your team will create possibilities. Start with the question: "What if people had donut jobs?" and take it from there.

Examine your standards and policies. Do they still fit the purpose for which they were created? Think about third industrial revolution forces and technologies and consider how they may change the way policies and standards are applied. For example, a CIO I know created a portal where staff could rate laptops used by people in the company. When people wanted a new laptop, they visited the portal and soon gravitated to the highest-rated devices. No standards were needed at all. This is consensus thinking, and it can be applied across the organization.

The key here is not to lament the flawed schooling system, but rather to learn from it, and apply those lessons in your organization.

NOTES

1 John Hagel, *Scaling Edges: How to Radically Transform Your Organization*, Idea Bite Press, 2014.
2 Charles Handy, *The Second Curve: Thoughts on Reinventing Society*, Random House Books, New York, 2016.
3 Erik Brynjolfsson, Andrew McAfee, Michael Sorell, and Feng Zhu, Scale without Mass: Business Process Replication and Industry Dynamics, *Harvard Business School Working Knowledge*, 2006. https://hbswk.hbs.edu/item/scale-without-mass-business-process-replication-and-industry-dynamics, [Accessed March 2019].

CHAPTER THREE

Generations in the workplace as a challenge for the C-Suite

There are three generations in the current workforce: baby boomers, Generation X, and millennials. Each generation was born in successive 20-year periods starting in about 1946. Classifying a group of people according to dates of birth over 20 years is, of course, a broad and sometimes problematic generalization. Researchers can only agree on the rough timeline and on general characteristics for each generation. Even then, some argue for splitting each generation into early and later groups, and there is some merit in that. However, the three generations do show specific characteristics, and it is useful to consider these when we look at the challenges facing the C-Suite. There are the conservative elders, the energetic leaders, and the non-conformist "digital natives." Executives in the C-Suite (mostly the dynamic leaders) have to examine themselves and their attitudes and behaviors while considering the elders and the non-conformists and the impacts that these have on their organizations. Indeed, there are old non-conformists and younger conservatives who distrust technology, but an analysis of generational classifications does help in identifying the three types of people (and all shades in between) and allows executives to think about strategies to manage and motivate their staff. So let's get started.

A recent study of 20,800 leaders[1] shows that they are made up of 18% baby boomers, 62% Generation X, and 20% millennials. Each generation was born in a roughly 20-year period, one following the other. Their attitudes to and their expectations of work differ significantly.

Given that the majority of organizational leaders are Generation X, with the elders in the C-Suite being baby boomers, and the majority of the workforce being millennials, it's appropriate to examine each of these demographic groups in more detail. Specifically, we need to look at the characteristics of each group as they pertain to their attitudes to work and authority, their ways of thinking, and their relationships with others. There are many conflicting views of the different generations, and I have taken the most commonly espoused views to illustrate their workplace beliefs and behaviors.

BABY BOOMERS

Baby boomers were born between 1946 and 1964 and named after the boom in the US population after World War II. They came of age when Beatles music was popular, rock and roll was an expression of their identity, and they listened to it on transistor radios. They went through the hippie period and many were in the civil rights and feminist movements. They were the first generation to grow up with television. The cold war was in full swing and the threat of nuclear war was always present. As a result, they were the first generation to believe that the world could end. They also generally avoided long-term planning for their demise. Moreover, they experienced the first intimation that climate change would be an issue in the future. More than 60% suffered financial loss during the economic crisis of 2007/2008, 42% have delayed retirement, and 25% are still working. They value loyalty, work ethic, a steady career path, and compensation appropriate to work done.

Marketing came of age as the baby boomers, with their disposable income, became the subjects of targeted marketing campaigns. They are also sometimes called "Generation Jones" because of their habit of "keeping up with the Joneses." They also experienced the first walk on the moon and woke up to the possibilities of technology and science. When late baby boomers started work, PCs were starting to be used in organizations and fiber-optics was a nascent technology. Barcodes were first used in 1974, and the concept of global warming became known to the world. In 1989, the world-wide-web came of age, along with Internet-based viruses. It was only in 1997 that the first truly portable cell-phones became widely available. Baby boomers have seen dramatic growth in technologies over their working careers and have had to grapple with immature and often unstable technologies introduced into their workplaces. As a result, they are often conservative when it comes to technology. An often-stated comment of baby boomers is: "I don't know much about technology, but I know it costs too much."

GENERATION X

Generation X was born between 1965 and 1980. There was an increase in divorce rates and a shift from a focus on the nuclear family (two parents and their kids) to a focus on adults and their need to self-actualize. Single parent families grew as a family unit and Generation X people were often latchkey children – with no adult supervision between the end of the school day and the time when the parent came home. Vacation times extended the latchkey period. Without an adult presence, latchkey children became more peer-oriented than the previous generation. They also grew a keener sense of internal locus of control – they believed that they made things happen rather than having things happen to them. The prevailing social conditions granted girls more opportunities, and Generation X children are regarded as the least racist.[2] They were also the first children to have access to computers in their homes and schools and are tech-savvy. They have higher ambitions than the previous generation and were primarily responsible for initiating tech startup companies.[3] Four out of five new companies were mainly the work of Generation X people. They started Google, Amazon, YouTube, and Wikipedia. Generation X are independent, resourceful, self-managing, adaptable, cynical, pragmatic, and are often skeptical of authority.[4] They do not seek the limelight[5] and do volunteer work more than any previous generations. They favor job satisfaction, individual advancement, and stability.

MILLENNIALS

Millennials are the generation born between the early 1980s and the late 1990s. They take their name from the fact that children of this generation would either be graduating from high school at the turn of the century or would be entering the new millennium as adults. This generation is noted particularly for their use of technology, and they are sometimes called "digital natives" because of their familiarity with technology and their ability to "speak tech." Younger millennials primarily use digital technologies for interpersonal communication. Millennials are highly educated and culturally diverse, more so than other generations.

Millennials are seen to be confident and tolerant, but also may have a sense of entitlement and narcissism. *Time Magazine* called them the "Me, me, me, generation." While they regard themselves as special, they are team-oriented and achievement-focused. They are the first generation to have significant student loan debt or to experience unemployment upon leaving school. Many millennials cannot afford to move away from the parental home. They exhibit "pragmatic idealism" with a sincere desire to make the world a better place but differ from previous generations in that they believe the way to do so is to replace old institutions with new ones, rather than to improve existing foundations. They volunteer more than any previous generation.

Millennials prefer a flat and informal organizational structure with a fair work-life balance. They want meaningful work, to be rewarded for their contribution, and to be creative. They prefer a close and informal relationship with supervisors, expect a free flow of information, and want immediate feedback. They value mentors and advice. They anticipate being involved in decision-making. They like flexibility and versatility in the workplace. They are not loyal to organizations unless that organization advances their careers, but they are often loyal to particular people in those organizations. They are not wedded to a specific career path and will go where the work is meaningful and engaging. Sixty percent of millennials would take a pay cut to pursue their passion.[6] When engaged, they take personal responsibility for solving problems and getting results even if it means crossing boundaries and breaking the rules. They are good collaborators and work well in teams, and volunteer for extra work provided it interests them.

For organizations, a summary of these three generations would look like this: baby boomers are the elders in an organization and are often outgoing executives with conservative attitudes to work. Generation X people make up a significant portion of management and leadership in organizations, and their worldviews and decision making affect the organization profoundly. They have seen technology blossom but have had to deal with its incorporation into organizations and their impacts on the way we work. Finally, millennials are digitally astute workers with high expectations of the organization to accommodate their ways of thinking and working. They expect to be challenged and to be creative.

THE GENERATION CHALLENGE

The challenges for executives in the C-Suite are numerous. Given that the majority of C-Suite members are Generation X, they need to examine their own beliefs and behaviors for where these differ from other generations.

While Generation X executives have an active internal locus of control, they need to accommodate baby boomers with their expectation of a steady career path, which they expected to be managed by others. Generation X independence contrasts with a Millennial's anticipation of working in teams and their need for mentoring and advice. Generation X executives expect to make independent decisions, while millennials expect to be involved in decisions.

When baby boomers started work, they expected to enter stable organizations and anticipated promotions if they performed well. People were paid for their time on the job rather than for delivering business outcomes. The baby boomer workplace was authoritarian, centrally controlled and deeply structured. They often distrust technology and respect decisions taken by superiors. For millennials, almost the opposite is true. They expect their workplace to be dynamic, constantly changing and challenging, engaging, and informal. They anticipate rewards for the results they achieve and will break the rules to achieve these results. They distrust decisions taken without them, especially if it concerns them, and they regard technology as an essential part of their working lives. Generation X (the majority of managers) are understandably somewhere in the middle. The problem is that they have to mediate the other two generations, with the emphasis being on millennials because they constitute the majority of the workforce.

The question of stability is a troubling one for Generation X executives. They need both stability and change in their organizations. Millennials are much more likely to value difference and provided they are challenged by it, they relish the opportunity of dealing with chaotic situations even if it means breaking the rules. So, the course of action is clear – delegate changing parts of the business to millennials and ensure that baby boomers are in the stable parts of the company.

Perhaps one of the first things for executives to do is to set up interest groups. A group could unpack generational differences and provide options for addressing them. One group might look at technology and how it can assist both customers and staff. Another could think about the future and how it might affect the organization and customers. One group should look at the way people work now and how it can be improved. Having representatives from each generation in each of these groups will widen perspectives and increase possibilities. These groups need to have teeth though, they cannot be a sideline to the decision-making process, nor can they be merely talk-shops.

Consider setting up an "elders council." They bring wisdom and ethical insight, but of course, they are also often conservative, and if not mandated correctly, may put a brake on developments. A converse council of "bright young minds" could bring new and often radical ideas to the table. These councils differ from interest groups in that they are age-specific, and their job is to provide insights from their age perspective. These councils cannot be allowed to become dissent factories, so they must be assigned specific tasks that are important to the organization. If they are on track, then they must be heeded.

The way millennials work is different. They are always connected, use their applications, collaborate freely, and expect challenging and interesting work. As a result, you may have policies in place that hinder their performance and productivity. Most organizations have BYOD (Bring your own device) policies, but do you have a "use your own applications" policy? Having people use their own applications is difficult for organizations as they have large, well-run, and integrated applications that they need staff to use. Otherwise, there will be different versions of the truth, missing data, and possibly whole sections of work that is below the company's radar at best, or illegal or non-compliant at worst. These hidden but useful applications are called "Shadow IT," and bedevil most organizations today. People use them (and not only millennials) because they find organizational systems cumbersome or unnecessarily bureaucratic or pedantic, or they find it difficult to get approval for their application. So they get their work done quietly on their own applications. There are ways of dealing with shadow IT, which will be too detailed to go through here. If you are interested, please visit the website "Reinventing the C-Suite"[7] for a blog post that deals with this subject.

The "way we work" challenge for C-Suite executives is two-fold: They should not expect others to work the way they do, and they should accommodate different ways of working. Neither problem is as easy to resolve as it sounds. I deal with this in Chapter 5, but for now, let's say that executives should examine how they and their predecessors have encoded a particular way of work into the DNA of the organization in its policies, procedures, governance, best practices, and indeed, in its culture. The important thing is that technology can change pretty much everything about how we work. Do you need meetings, process flows, authorizations, an IT department (or any "department" for that matter), or even that many staff?

Work ethic attitudes differ for each generation. All will work hard, but their motivation is different. Baby boomers are more "nine-to-five" workers and expect to work from a fixed location, Generation X will work until the job is done, while millennials will work while they are engaged and interested. This seems to be a sound mix of work styles, but tensions will arise when there's work to be done and approaches to work differ.

Career progression expectations also differ. The first generation expects a steady path to be mapped out, the second will do what they need to progress, and the third is quite happy to bounce from job to job to follow their interest. Millennials expect rewards for competency, not titles, which, in their self-assured way, they do not take seriously.

Decision-making styles differ: baby boomers believe that meetings will result in decisions, Generation X has an entrepreneurial mindset, so decide and act, and millennials want to be consulted on decisions.

The differences between generations are, of course, an abstraction. All generational attitudes and types are in each age-group. However, thinking about distinct generational perspectives, approaches to work, and reactions to authority can help executives develop plans to deal with them.

NOTES

1 DDI, CB, EYGM, *Global Leadership Forecast 2018*, Development Dimensions International Inc, The Conference Board Inc., EYGM Limited, 2018. www.ddiworld.com/DDI/media/trend-research/glf2018/global-leadership-forecast-2018_ddi_tr.pdf?ext=.pdf, [Accessed November 2019].
2 William Strauss, *What Future Awaits Today's Youth in the New Millennium?* Angelo State University, San Angelo, TX, 2015. www.angelo.edu/events/university_symposium/97_Strauss.php, [Accessed April 2019].
3 Margot Hornblower, Great Xpectations of So-Called Slackers, *Time Magazine*, June 9, 1997. http://content.time.com/time/subscriber/article/0,33009,986481,00.html, [Accessed April 2019].
4 Doug and Polly White, *What to Expect From Gen-X and Millennial Employees*, 2014. www.entrepreneur.com/article/240556, [Accessed April 2019].
5 Jeff Gordinier, X Saves the World: How Generation X Got the Shaft but Can Still Keep Everything from Sucking, *Viking Adult*, March 27, 2008. ISBN 978-0670018581.
6 Morley Winograd and Michael Hais, *How Millennials Could Upend Wall Street and Corporate America*, Brookings Institution, Washington, WA, November 30, 2001.
7 www.terrygrey.com/post/accommodating-shadow-it-in-a-nice-way.

CHAPTER FOUR

Information inputs as a challenge to the C-Suite

In Chapter 1 we looked at information as a source of power for executives. The free flow of information is counteracting this form of control, but this is not the only challenge to executives. The critical problem is that there's an excessive amount of data available to organizations, much of which they are not even aware, or if they are, they are not leveraging to their advantage. So, ensuring that it is identified, sorted, and organized so that it is meaningful for the business is a critical role for the C-Suite.

Back in 1993, management guru Warren Bennis talked about the difference between leadership and management.[1] Put simply, he said that leaders manage meaning, attention, self, and trust – I use the mnemonic "MAST" for what leaders do. Bennis said that managers plan, organize, execute, and monitor – here I use "POEM" to help me remember.

The management of meaning is a vital role and skill for leaders. There's too much data available to organizations, and leaders need to assign organizational meaning to it so that it can be useful. The meaning of some data for a charity will be different from the meaning of the same data for a business. Moreover, a logistics business will find some data helpful, while a tech company will see the usefulness in other data. So data becomes information when it is contextualized. Executives set the context for their organization, and herein lies a risk because that context relies on the lens through which they view events. In Chapter 3 we saw how different generations have different "lenses" through which they see the world, the workplace, authority, decisions, and many other elements of their lives, and their interpretation of what they see and how they see it is likely to be informed by their attitudes and beliefs. The problem is that everyone in the organization has access to the same data (if they want it), and their interpretation is likely to differ from some executives. This is where the management of attention comes in. If an executive cannot direct the attention of the entire organization to act on the way they interpret information, then people will choose their own direction. One definition of a leader is someone who sees the same things as others but understands it differently and can get others to support their interpretation and act on it.

INFORMATION IN CONTEXT

Information is in the middle of the data/information/knowledge/wisdom stack. Data are facts (for example, it is 30°C outside). Information is contextual – 30°C could be hot in England, or pleasantly cool in Rydah. Knowledge is linked to action – we know that 30°C is hot for our customers, so we should sell more ice-cream today. Wisdom has a value orientation – should we copy the recipe from our competitor? Figure 4.1 shows the stack.

However, this figure leaves out the subjectivity that is applied through the lenses of the multiple participants in the chain from data through to wisdom. Figure 4.2 represents the data stack when we think through organizational lenses.

How we apply context to data depends on our worldview. Newspapers often report on events (particularly political events) through a particular lens. This is no different for organizations: A start-up company will see data through an "opportunity" lens while an established corporate may view the same data through a "competitive threat" lens. The start-up is looking for where they can grow, while the corporate is seeing what it must defend – the

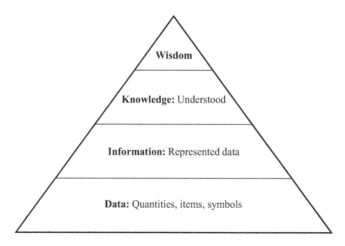

Figure 4.1 The data-wisdom stack

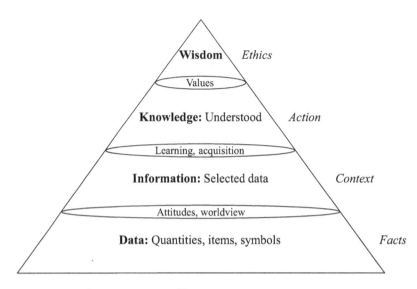

Figure 4.2 Applying organizational lenses

data is the same. So, the informational context for each will differ – some will see opportunities while others will see threats. To turn information into action, we need to acquire knowledge and understanding of what we see – what does the information mean? If the corporate understands that the data could represent a threat, given the way the information is contextualized, it may act to neutralize the threat. However, an executive with a different understanding of the information might choose to see opportunities and spin off a start-up to take advantage of the opportunities.

The area of wisdom is a troublesome one in today's digital environment. I was once talking to the CIO (Chief Information Officer) of a large corporation, and he was worried about the ethics of computing. He said: "Here we are using computers to speed up processes and production, which depletes the earth's resources faster than ever before." However, his ethical dilemma did not stop him from doing his job to the best of his abilities – speeding up the depletion of the earth's resources. Nicholas Carr,[2] in his book "The Glass Cage: How our Computers are Changing Us," examines the hidden costs of technology, showing how computers are taking something substantial from us – our identity, our engagement with the real world, and making us dissatisfied with life and ourselves. He ends the book with the observation that the technology and its application cannot be separated – if we have it, we will use it. Finally, he plaintively calls for wisdom in the application and use of technology. Unfortunately, wisdom is too often overruled by the profit motive, or by people wanting to keep their livelihood secure.

An example of data moving up the stack would be your customers telling you that they need to be able to check on the progress of their order on their mobile phones. In context, this data could be interpreted as merely being noise from customers who are always complaining, or it could be seen as an opportunity to improve our service and strengthen customer loyalty to our brand. How we act on the information depends on our interpretation, and we might stop communicating with demanding customers, or we might give them their new app. Even the latter approach could have adverse effects, as customers might start querying why their order spent so long in dispatch. Wisdom is required to value this feedback as an opportunity to improve the logistics process.

Internal information as an input to organizations comes from many sources. Typically, executives look to their information systems, which is the immediately apparent source. However, they should be aware of the sugar-coating effect that often pertains to organizations that are centrally controlled, over-authoritarian or where fear is in play. The fear may be mild alarm, as in: "She won't like this information," or may be real, as in: "I could lose my job here." Each successive layer in the hierarchy may sugar-coat information to put the best light on it, leaving out contrary data or softening the blow by averaging the effects or de-emphasizing unpleasant news. By the time the executive sees the report, things may look fine or only mildly worrying. Internal sources of information could be problematic if the sugar-coating effect is active, but internal information is only a small portion of what you, your customers, your staff, and your competition know. One form of internal information is seldom tapped – the knowledge inside your staff's heads. This knowledge leaves the organization every night or goes for good when the staff member resigns. Some organizations provide internal databases and collaboration tools, but often these are disorganized – the industry calls this "content chaos." There is not much point in getting information out of people's heads into databases if no-one can find it.

A helpful concept is the Johari window, which is used in self-development and organization behavior circles. Its use has been extended to business to analyze what we know and do not know about ourselves, and what others (for example, customers, competitors, and staff) know or do not know about us. In the Johari window, what you know about yourself and others (your customers, suppliers, and competition) is essential, but equally what your customers know about your organization (marketing) is useful. In the past "inside-out" perspectives were used to design products and services asking questions like: "What can we make, and who will buy it?" In these digital, freely flowing information days it is more important to use "outside-in" thinking: "Who is out there and what might they want our organization to supply them?" Therefore, information that exists outside the organization is crucial for developing a picture of the potential demand for your services, for finding problems that your customers have and solving them, and for keeping an eye on competitors. It is the role of the executive to find this information and to make sense of it for the organization.

In seeking inputs from the outside world, customer surveys and focus groups may be useful, but often non-partisan information can be much more valuable and informative and can help the organization build new products and services. There are classic cases of product failures because businesses depended on inside information or indeed on surveys. The Ford Edsel was a car built for $400 million (that's $3.5 billion in today's terms), but Ford customers didn't want it. They wanted smaller, more fuel-efficient cars, but no-one asked them.

Coca-Cola did ask their customers and developed New Coke, a sweeter drink designed to compete directly with Pepsi. In focus groups, customers liked the taste but thought it would take some getting used to. They were asked if they would buy the product if it were Coke, and some said they would, but some became upset and said they would stop drinking Coke altogether. Executives at Coke were determined to launch the sweeter product and conducted external surveys that supported their views. What Coke did not do was ask customers if they would buy New Coke if it replaced "Old Coke" completely. This is where Coke messed it up. They received over 40,000 calls and letters of complaint, one letter was addressed to the "Chief Dodo, The Coca-Cola Company," and another asking for the autograph of the executive in charge of the change as he was: "one of the dumbest executives in American business history." The mistake was to ignore the focus group feedback because it didn't confirm the Coke executives' pre-conceived expectations, and to give credence to the survey because it supported what they wanted – they were guilty of confirmation bias. There are many other examples: Frito-Lay introducing a fat-free potato chip that acted as a laxative, Coors trying to sell bottled water to their customers who wanted beer, smokeless cigarettes that worked – because they went out, and the Microsoft Zune which was meant to compete with the iPod and didn't.

All of these are examples of executives thinking "inside-out" or not believing contrary data. Moreover, all of them are associated with executives' attitudes and opinions. In the digital world, inside-out thinking and untested beliefs are dangerous. Imagine what would happen with a "new Coke" debacle with social media being the primary communication medium. There would have been resignations and not merely a hurried re-launch of Classic Coke. The CEO and founder of Uber suffered in social media circles over allegations of sexual misconduct and discrimination, but when it was announced that he would join President Trump's economic advisory council, the #DeleteUber campaign resulted in 200,000 deletions of the app, and he resigned as CEO. All of this was because of untested allegations and news that something might happen. The freedom of information in the connected world means that executives cannot ignore the outside environment and its influencers, and also that they need to mind their behavior. Thinking in Johari window terms, what others know about you will undoubtedly be broadcast.

Information is required for the development of strategies, products, services, and the tactics needed to respond to events. Much of this information cannot be gathered from internal sources, so the C-Suite has to look outside. Sometimes a media monitoring service can prove useful, especially if they track social media, but that only addresses about 10% of the issue – finding out what people are saying about your organization. You need to get information on potential customer requirements, on trends that your organization can exploit, and on what your competitors are doing. Some organizations select "friendly" customers and give them discounts or promotional deals to get them to share their and their associates' requirements. A friendly customer is a powerful thing, as many organizations test MVPs with them. MVPs are Minimal Viable Products – new products with only enough features to satisfy customers with a useful service. Developing MVPs is a way of minimizing investment in new products until you are sure that people want and will use them. This avoids mistakes, as even if the customer doesn't want the MVP, you have learned something, which means that you have acquired knowledge about what customers do and don't want.

In the digital age, there is another way of gathering information. The Internet of Things (IoT) has come of age. IoT involves using the internet to connect to everyday devices or specially installed devices like cameras or sensors to collect data from the real world. IoT devices can cost as little as 60c, and the cost is dropping. Because so much data is collected, most IoT initiatives are accompanied by artificial intelligence programs that interpret the data and present it in a digestible form. However, we're getting too technical here. The point is that information is getting easier to collect, and executives need to make use of this development. Their role is not to collect data, but it is to derive meaning, either positive or negative, from the data available to them. They also have to obtain meaning from this data to provide contextual leadership to the organization.

Another source of information is in the organization's ecosystem. Your suppliers and even competitors can give you information that can have meaning for your business.

There is, of course, the danger of information and sensory overload, and it is the executive's role to filter information for the organization.

Probably the first task for the C-Suite is to look at how and through what processes the organization senses its environment. Then they need to look at whether these "senses" need sharpening. After that, they need to look at how that information is organized. Once organized, executives can set about establishing meaning inherent in the information – this is the primary tool for avoiding sensory overload in the organization. Some executives write "position papers," which, on one page, states whether a particular trend has meaning or not and why they believe this to be so. They are then able to show people that they've thought about something and taken a considered position on it. It's not a hard habit to establish.

Do a Johari exercise for the organization: Examine what you know about yourselves (and how you know it to be true), think about what others know about you, and importantly evaluate what your organization does not know and how you can come to understand it.

Another action for the C-Suite is to take an honest look at their data-viewing lenses and identify the attitudes and assumptions which create these lenses. This exercise can sometimes lead to strident debates, but the resultant clarity should benefit executives and their organizations.

NOTES

1 Warren Bennis, *Learning Some Basic Truisms about Leadership in the New Business Paradigm*, G.P. Putnam & Sons, New York, 1993.
2 Nicholas Carr, *The Glass Cage: How Our Computers are Changing Us*, W.W. Norton, New York, 2014. ISBN-10: 0393351637.

CHAPTER FIVE

Digital transformation and its effects on the organization

Estimates differ about the size of the internet being between 5 billion and 50 billion searchable pages. The average size of a web page is about 6.5 printed pages. So, if you wanted to "print the internet," you would need a minimum of 33 billion pages. That's about a billion books, which would require 100 million bookshops to hold them (not that there would be many buyers, because most of the internet is free). The argument here is between "digitization and bricks and mortar" or as author Negroponte put it, between "bits and atoms." Essentially data is infinite, and physical constituents take up space – imagine where you would put 100 million bookshops. Even if we put in as many for all the people on Earth, as you find in Buenos Aires, which has the most bookshops per capita in the world, we would still need to find space for 99 million bookshops.

Technology allows businesses and people to achieve "scale without mass" – IT allows businesses to extend their services and product offerings to their customers wherever they are without needing to build branches or ally with agents – but technology is merely the enabler. Charlene Li[1] says that it is behaviors that cause disruption, not technology. If people like and use the technology, their behavior will change, and that is what drives disruption. She says that digital transformation needs an anchor, and that is the "very dynamic digital customer." And there you have it – technologies that cause behavioral changes cause disruption. If people hadn't changed their behavior around searching for things online, we would probably need those 100 million bookshops if we wanted to duplicate all the data that was available on the internet. However, people did change their behavior, and in many other areas as well: They use social networking; use apps rather than dealing with clerks and salespeople; they expect 24/7 service from banks; and they call for taxi services on their mobiles. The list goes on.

In this chapter, we will look at the significant technologies responsible for behavior changes and are consequently becoming disruptive technologies. We'll only look at a selection that affects business operations and their interactions with customers – to discuss all technologies would take many chapters, and by the time it's written the game will have moved on. Firstly though, we need to take a step back: What is digital and its associated derivative words like digitization and digitalization?

WHAT IS DIGITAL?

"Digital" is as advertised – a series of zeros and ones. This is a binary code consisting of only two digits, which can provide for a rich set of instructions and data that drives all things digital – music, applications, documents, and any other item that is processed by a computer. As a side issue, biocomputers, which use DNA or proteins, which provide much more computing power than binary code, could change the face of computing, increasing speed and complexity by many multiples of ten. They work in parallel where mechanical computers are serial devices, they are much more energy-efficient, and they can self-replicate. All of these are exciting and perhaps disturbing developments, but the technology is very sophisticated, and only conceptual biocomputers have been made. Similarly, Quantum computing which uses quantum mechanical principles to code data can be 100 million times faster than bit driven computers and could revolutionize computing. However, like biocomputers, this technology is still in its infancy. So while this is interesting, at the moment, we need to look at serial, mechanical computers, which are powerful in their own right.

Digital is the state of something represented as binary code. Digitization is the process of getting that something (paper documents, images, sound, and so on) into a digital state. Digitalization is the enabling, transforming or automating of digitized data. It also means the enabling of behaviors that use digital processes. So you can't digitize people (turn them into ones and zeros), but you can digitalize them – enable them to use digitized data and processes.

Digital transformation is a sweeping term used to describe the digitization and the digitalization of processes in such a way that behavior changes in a transformative way. However, as Charlene Li says, the behavior is the key, not the digitalization.

THERE ARE FOUR MAIN TYPES OF DIGITALIZATION THAT AFFECT THE BUSINESS WORLD:

- The devices and software that enable digital processes – this would include computers, networks, mobile devices, wearable devices, and the software that runs them. Platforms are a construct that combines many technologies into a seemingly single "instrument" that can be used by people, for example, Facebook, Amazon, Twitter, and so on.
- Media and content: Media such as music, video, and photos include media platforms such as Instagram, YouTube, Google Maps, and so on, which allow the use of media, interaction, and commentary at the same time. Content encompasses digitized documents such as books and news that can be delivered to devices that use digital data such as mobiles, computers, and indeed cinemas. Search engines also fit into this category.
- Industry, which includes all digitalized processes, interfaces, applications, devices, and tools that businesses, governments, NGOs, and any organization that transacts with the public or with each other.
- Culture. This is a contentious issue as it depends on all of the above forms of digitalization, but its effect has been so profound on cultural aspects of our lives, including being the primary descriptor of Millennials that it deserves its own category. It affects the way people behave, work, see the world, and interact with it.

Clearly, each category crosses into others and crosses the artificial boundaries suggested by the above shortlist, but these definitions will suit us for the moment.

TECHNOLOGY AND BUSINESS

Many technologies affect businesses now and will affect operations shortly. We'll look at a few of them, more to get a flavor of the types of disruption that could challenge C-Suite thinking, than to document all tech that is changing the business world. One of the proposals in Part 2 is that the C-Suite should have a role that scans technology developments and trends and understands what such technologies mean for the organization. This overview may seem simple to tech-savvy readers, but many executives are not particularly proficient in technological matters, and I hope to give a sense of the types of technology that can dramatically change (or have changed) the organizational and competitive landscape.

The first significant device to influence the way business worked was the PC or personal computer. Before that time, computers were large central devices with many screens connected to it. A PC allowed individuals to run their own programs, rather than those on the central processor (or mainframe – a somewhat obsolete term now). Initially, the primary software run by individuals on PCs was the spreadsheet – VisiCalc being the first brand. PC based spreadsheets were modeled after paper spreadsheets and were the reason given for the purchase of the majority of business PCs in those early days, and VisiCalc was named the first "Killer App."

The portable PC, or laptop, became a useful device in organizations in 1993, but sales were low compared to desktops, and only exceeded desktop sales in about 2008. Now, portable computers include tablets and smartphones. The effect of mobile computing on the way people and organizations work has been dramatic. People work from where they are at a time that suits them. Customers operate in the same style and expect to interact with suppliers from anywhere and at any time. For instance, if there is a long line at a ticket stall, a customer will want to buy tickets online and skip the queue.

While personal devices empower customers and workers, the real power for organizations lies in larger computers. Initially, companies used mainframes – computers with high speeds and enormous computing power. However, the growth of servers has risen recently, and they are a vital component of organizational computing today. Mainframes are used by large organizations for critical applications and bulk processing. Servers are essentially large and stable PCs that typically service one type of organizational activity (for example, printing, applications, communications, and catalogs). Cloud computing allows organizations to access remote computers via their networks. Cloud computing has several benefits – it enables organizations to move from CapEx to Opex spending regimes, improves security and quality, allows for automatic software updates, provides for disaster recovery, and enhances the flexibility of organizational computing. However, the Cloud can also increase complexity and may cost more (usually because the in-house computing is of lower quality with less security than the cloud solution).

A form of computing that will have a striking effect on organizational computing is IoT or the Internet of Things. This class of computing connects any devices which have processing power via the internet to a central computing facility. This facility collects and analyzes data from wherever it comes and allows for decisions (usually automated decisions) to be made. For example, devices include smartphones or GPS devices that can track movement and then update traffic flow data and present it back to the instrument. So, if you are in a traffic jam, the central facility will use data gathered from your device and others, deduce that these devices are all stationary or slow-moving, tell you and others that traffic is backed up in your location, and predict how long the delay will be. Different uses of IoT are for drive-in fast food outlets which assess how long the queue is and change the available menu items, prepare meals faster, and thus reduce the queue length. IoT is primarily a "sense and respond" technology, but it is also used to analyze large tranches of data to help organizations improve their operations. One of the important uses of IoT is in manufacturing to improve efficiencies and throughputs. IoT and other technologies used in manufacturing are often called "Industrie 4.0" because the methods and technologies were initially developed in Germany but have been adopted by many economies since then.

There are, of course, many technologies and devices that will change the nature of business operations and indeed change the business model radically, and there are more in development every day. The speed of change is the issue for executives today, more than the technologies and behaviors driving that change. Executives must be able to track and identify meaningful changes, understand how changes will affect their organization and their customers, make rapid decisions, and implement a response to the change as quickly as possible.

DIGITAL MEDIA IN BUSINESS

Chapter 4 deals with information inputs as a challenge to the C-Suite. These inputs are all digital and are mostly driven by content, which is relatively structured data. Media (pictures and video) is unstructured data and is significantly more challenging to analyze, and at the moment are relatively complex and hence may be impractical. Machines can count objects in images, analyze tones and colors, and do some reasonably sophisticated pattern recognition such as face recognition, but that's about it. The science of image recognition is advancing quickly, though. People are a different proposition altogether. Their image recognition abilities are staggeringly advanced, but it will be years before computers can match us.

Websites, for instance, have evolved from web 1.0 – a static, readable version, to web 2.0 – a more dynamic, writable version. The first type of site presents information which can be read by customers; the second type encourages interaction between people – Facebook, Wiki, and any site where users can contribute. This type of site is appropriate for getting feedback from customers. Many websites use cookies, which track your activity and any information that you volunteer and pass these onto monitoring software, or your browser, to make your browsing easier. Web 3.0 is executable – it contains algorithms that can customize the site for specific types of users, or particular users if it knows who the user is. Google Search is a good example that customizes searches based on your previous history of using the facility. Tivo is a television assistant, searching for programs based on your preferences. While Web 3.0 is the one in use today, there is talk of Web 4.0, which does not have a name yet, but might be called the assistant web. Search engines won't disappear, but they are more likely to be included in a personal digital assistant (PDA), which understands your language and searches for answers for you in the background. Examples already exist like Siri, Cortana, Alexa, and many others. They understand your speech and are improving their understanding all the time. One can ask one's PDA what the weather will be like tomorrow in Rome, and it will search the internet and tell you in a sentence or two.

Inside organizations, intelligent "bots" are being implemented. They are programs that are powered by artificial intelligence and machine learning which converse with customers and staff. The generic term for internal robotic applications is RPA (Robotic Process Automation). Executives would use RPA where rules-based, high volume, and routine processes can be replaced or assisted by artificial intelligence programs. These processes include actioning regular queries, performing standard calculations, and maintaining data. For instance, RPA could handle questions from customers that are quickly answered like: "What is the status of my order?" or, "Where is your nearest branch?" The artificial intelligence would try to learn from such queries and anticipate customer questions. Other uses are in accounting (transaction reporting, budgeting), financial services (foreign exchange payments, account monitoring), healthcare (patient records, claims, billing, analysis), human resources (onboarding, updating employee information), and supply chain (monitoring inventory, tracking shipments, processing payments). As you can see, most of the tasks are unglamorous and somewhat dull, and the use of RPA frees staff up for more complex and exciting work. In general, people appreciate the assistance.

Media and content affect business operations significantly. For instance, your website cannot be a static information delivery system. That is merely the first step in your customer interaction. The emphasis is on bi-directional communication, so executives need to think about what kinds of communication would be useful to both the customer and the organization. It's relatively commonplace to allow customers to raise queries and make complaints, but "outside-in" thinkers would run surveys and competitions soliciting the views of customers on, for example, what your next product should be, or if there was one product they could upgrade, what would it be? You're trying to get a view on what customers are thinking and what they want, as well as commenting on or even complaining about your products and services. Websites are not merely words and information – they should also educate and even entertain. The use of videos and podcasts is growing, and many organizations provide resources for customers to use. For instance, a roofing company could offer tips and techniques for minor roof repairs, maintenance, and painting. This company knows that if customers and potential customers visit their site to find out about all matters concerning roofs, then when the time comes for significant repairs or a new roof, people will look to them for answers. They know that by giving something, they will be seen to be a trusted supplier. Some companies also compare their products and prices with their competitors, even suggesting that customers use their competitors if their product does fit the requirements of their customers. This builds customer confidence and promotes repeat visits. The use of technology is more than an extension of your sales force. It allows you to educate, help, and please customers. Importantly, behind the scenes, it will enable you to track your customers' visits and interactions and to track their journey with your organization. Technology is an excellent silo-breaker: Your sales team might be excellent, but your customers' journey involves onboarding and opening accounts, delivery of your services, managing the quality of their experience, dealing with your finance department, and any touch-point with your organization. Your technology is involved in every stage of that journey, so you should use it to track customer journeys.

Instant messaging, collaboration tools, online planners, project team tools, and to-do lists should change the way people work totally. However, people haven't altered their work behaviors to the extent allowed by the technologies available. In theory, email should be a seldom-used tool, but of course, it isn't. Instant messaging and sharing and communal editing of documents should relegate email to the formal business letter that we saw in the past. Instant messaging (IM) is more than a short one-on-one chat – most IM tools allow for tracking of conversations and for asynchronous communication. Synchronous communication is involved in meetings, phone calls, and any device where you don't hang up before receiving a reply – it is a direct connection, while asynchronous communication happens with a time lag – email being the most common form, but all texting tools are also asynchronous. Modern communication tools allow for much more efficient asynchronous communication through message boards and online forums. In a business context, a particular application (say a team collaboration app) would have a workflow function, shared documents, message boards, shared calendars, a chat function, possibly an online meeting function, and a reminder service. Who needs email? However, people's behavior hasn't changed significantly in the use of collaborative tools, which would suggest that this is not a transformative technology (yet).

Online meetings have fundamentally changed businesses, both in how much their staff travels and in terms of how often they meet. In the past, international meetings were few in number and involved wasted days in travel. Now, someone in Europe can start the day with discussions with people in Australia, Japan, and China, move to Europe, the Middle East, and Africa, and finish with the Americas – all in a standard working day. Depending on where the meetings are held, online meetings tend to save about 95% of the cost of a meeting but also speed up communications which enable faster iteration of plans and developments. They improve productivity in non-meeting times and finally provide improved work experience. Following Charlene Li's suggestion, the changed behavior of people has made online meetings a disruptive technology.

Combining collaboration tools and online meetings with stable, fast, and secure internet access has, more than ever, allowed people to work from home. Which, as we will see in the next chapter, fundamentally changes the workplace, its hierarchy, the nature of jobs and roles, and ultimately the business model. According to International Workspace Group (IWG plc),[2] more than 50% of employees work half the week away from their offices. Key technology considerations include access to secure printing and scanning facilities and insufficient cybersecurity. While 55% of the technology used is paid for by the company, only 28% of companies help their staff financially in setting up home offices. But there is no doubt that technology has disrupted workspaces and working habits forever. I'll talk about how those workplaces and work habits have changed in the next chapter, but it is sufficient to note here that technology has created improved working conditions and performance for almost every business.

TECHNOLOGY CHANGES EVERYTHING IN BUSINESS

Technology makes the business environment and the business more efficient and productive. It changed the way we communicate with each other and our customers and makes organizations more relevant. As a pleasant spin-off, technology has made business operations more accurate and precise, and throughputs have increased exponentially.

However, technology has also changed our externally facing operations in the way we compete, react to business challenges, and scale businesses. Some examples include:

- In 2009 National Geographic's revenue had dropped steadily for ten years, but they struck a channel TV deal, reworked their websites, and used social media to communicate with audiences actively. Their revenue nearly trebled in four years.
- Another large retailer has an app that allows customers to compile their shopping list and add up the cost before leaving home. When they get to the store, the app guides them on the most efficient route through that particular store to each of their selected products.
- A washing powder manufacturer introduced a "smart peg" – a sensor that is placed on the washing line which detects light, humidity, and temperature. It has a Wi-Fi module that communicates with a smartphone, letting the person who hung the washing know when the weather changes.
- Some businesses use face recognition software to assess the gender and approximate the age of specific customers and to place adverts tailored to their demographic on screens near them.
- Augmented reality shops, interactive chocolate bars and soda cans, and apps that allow women to try on makeup virtually before buying – the list goes on.

These uses of technology may appear gimmicky, but if used by customers, and if they change buying behaviors, they could become disruptive to competitors.

We have dealt mainly with workplace and consumer-facing technologies, but "Industrie 4.0" is a technological revolution that is profoundly affecting the manufacturing and logistics industries. More and more manufacturing plants are using the Internet of Things (IoT), robotics, machine learning, and even blockchain concepts to allow them to operate small production runs to meet variable customer requirements. They use machine learning to drive efficiencies and anticipate demand. They use blockchain to track and verify payment of shipments. Robotics are used to work in repetitive and dull environments, and also to service areas where safety is an issue. A mine that had 2,000 workers underground was able to reduce this number to fewer than 50 with automation and was able to keep those 50 people in safe environments. We know about drones in use in military applications. However, drones are also being used on autonomous flights, monitoring traffic patterns, scanning agricultural lands, and conducting geological surveys. There are smart tractors which work the fields without a driver in attendance, brick-laying robots, Smart Cities which sense traffic and change traffic light cycles, 3-D printing of parts (I had a tooth implant manufactured in a 3-D printer), and predictive (and even prescriptive) analytics are all forms of Industrie 4.0.

Importantly, artificial intelligence and big data are now being used to evaluate business models and offer better models for consideration. The technology helps executives think, make decisions, compete, strategize, run their businesses, and drive change. It affects how people work, want to work, communicate, and define their success.

Technology is wonderful and terrible at the same time. It eases workloads but makes us busier than ever. It allows instant communication and swamps us with messages and demands for our time. It lets us look up anything at any time but compromises our ability to think and research. It shows us where we are but dampens our desire to explore. It gets us to our destination but short-circuits the journey. It calculates rapidly and flawlessly but dampens our mental processes. It gives jobs and takes jobs. We could go on here for a long time. However, it is not the technology itself that creates the dichotomy. Instead, it is how we use technology that is the issue. As we've seen, a technology that changes behaviors can be disruptive and it requires foresight to see the disruption coming and wisdom to ensure that these behavior changes are positive and beneficial to people. The role of the C-Suite is more than tracking, evaluating, and using technology. It also requires insight and enlightened contemplation.

NOTES

1 Charlene Li. *The Engaged Leader: A Strategy for Your Digital Transformation*, Wharton Digital Press, 2015.
2 *The IWG Global Workspace Survey, IWG Jersey*, March 2019. https://iwgplc.com/global-workspace-survey–2019, [Accessed July 2019].

CHAPTER SIX
The world of work

More than anything, technology has changed the way we work, how we interpret events, and how we interact with the world. It all started with the agricultural revolution and has shifted with every revolution since. I'll briefly cover the evolution of work, then move on to the current world of work and how it may challenge executives to accommodate how people expect their work environment to be structured.

A WORK RETROSPECTIVE

Before the Agricultural Revolution (circa 10000 BP) people "worked" by hunting wild animals and gathering seeds, fruits, and berries. This was labor-intensive and time-consuming work. A much easier plan was to collect seeds from food plants and sow them near a habitat. Over time, people selected the best seeds and replanted them, thus starting the process of selective breeding to improve yields, ripening times, and size. The same happened with animals, but they were selectively bred for their docility, size, and breeding characteristics, all of which increased food security and freed up time for other things. This was, of course, the Agricultural Revolution, which took place in various places in the world from 11000 BP in the Fertile Crescent, to about 4000 BP in America and sub-Saharan Africa. So, people worked at different activities – settlements became permanent, with all the work that was created by permanence, and people developed new tools, furniture, and artifacts, and specialization became commonplace. People were free to explore their world, and scientific, religious, and philosophical thought blossomed. Importantly, trade and accounting became necessary as specialized people or societies needed to trade their goods for products that they didn't grow or manufacture themselves. While the advances were many, the Agricultural Revolution wasn't all about progress. With the concentration of people in settled places, diseases abounded. The move to more cereal-based diets created vitamin deficiencies and bone disorders. Life expectancy and stature dropped, only to recover to pre-revolution figures in the twentieth century. Child labor was introduced, class-systems came into being, and central governments were constituted in the form of rulers, who produced little or nothing themselves, and so introduced taxation.

There were three other agricultural revolutions. The Arab Agricultural Revolution, from the eighth to the thirteenth century, introduced new crops and techniques to the Muslim world. This also coincided with the "Islamic Golden Age," which saw significant advances in technology, science, medicine, writing, government, law, and mathematics. From the 17th to the nineteenth centuries, the western world had another agricultural revolution, with increased agricultural productivity, and then from 1930 to 1960, the developing world experienced a revolution that increased yields and mechanization. Each revolution involved enhanced knowledge which was used to produce more with less – a trend that continues in all spheres of business.

The next economic revolution in the world of work happened during the Industrial Revolution. There have been four industrial revolutions, but the first probably introduced the most profound changes to the way people worked. Previously, manufacturing tended to be undertaken by hand, and with the introduction of steam and water power, this manufacturing was done by machines. Add a revolution in iron production and in chemical manufacturing and you had a recipe for mass production, but also for mass pollution, poor labor conditions, malnutrition, overcrowding, illness, inadequate water and sewage supply, and population concentration in poor living conditions. Gas lighting allowed factories and workshops to operate after dark and long work hours were the norm, typically 12 to 16 hours per day with only Sunday off. However, per capita income did increase, although the general standard of living improved noticeably only in the late nineteenth century. There was a growing middle class of engineers, clerks, businessmen, and foremen, for whom the standard of living did increase substantially, but they were in the minority.

Work changed. Before the industrial revolution, most of the workforce worked the land, either as self-employed farmers or as laborers. They spun their own yarn, wove material, and made their own clothes. By the sixteenth century, some of these activities had turned into cottage industries, creating material, clothing, furniture, and tools for other people. Merchants often provided raw materials, paid for work by items produced, and sold these to the public. The term "industry" was only becoming prevalent by the mid-1830s and was taken to mean the processing of raw materials and the manufacture of goods in factories. Interestingly, Adam Smith published his book "An Inquiry into the Nature and Causes of the Wealth of Nations" in 1776 before the term "industry" was in full use.

A typical workday during the industrial revolution was a grim affair. With a large pool of people wanting to work, employers could set wages as low as they wanted. Most workers were unskilled and earned a subsistence wage at best. Women received between one-third to half of the men's pay, and children received even less. There was only a break for lunch and dinner. Factories were grim places, poorly lit, dangerous, and smoky. People ended their workdays covered in soot, and accidents were commonplace. It is little wonder then that labor unions formed. They were preceded by guilds and were initially only for skilled workers, but by the 1830s there were increasing protests and withdrawal of work by laborers. Working conditions had slowly been improving, with children under the age of nine being banned from working from 1819 but this was seldom enforced, although the Factory Act in 1833 was more successful in prohibiting children from working and in limiting work hours for nine- to thirteen-year-olds to nine hours a day. Adults still worked more than 12 hours per day.

Today's world of work is so different from the industrial revolution working environment that surely no comparisons can be made. Yet, many of the assumptions that we have about how people work were formed during the industrial revolution and remain unchallenged today. In fact, these assumptions have become the lore, and sometimes, the law, around what work is, why people work, who does the work, and how, where, and when work is performed.

All of the old assumptions are up for grabs. Some assumptions about work have changed to the extent that people question why we did that before? For example, as late as the 1970's, we used to think that people should join an organization as a low-paid worker, work their way up through the ranks, and end up in senior management. Either way, it was a "job for life." In 1950, my dad finished Standard 8 and was at a school leaving age. His father marched him down the high street to get him a "proper job" – either in a bank or an insurance company, both were equally stable. The first company they came to was an insurance company, and my grandfather marched my dad up to the counter and said: "This boy has come to work for you!" That was how it was done in those days. My dad started as a "stamp-boy." His job was to collect all the letters being sent out, calculate how much postage was needed, collect the money from petty cash, buy stamps, put the stamps on the envelopes, and post them. Then do it all again the next day. He eventually became the General Manager in the insurance company and stayed there until he retired at the age of 56 because he hated every moment of his working career. That was a job for life.

Of course, we believed that men are the real workers and women should have the "soft" and "safe" jobs – like in offices or behind counters. Oh wait, we still believe that! Based on the numbers who participate, we think that women should not: be involved at the same level as men in industry, mining or fighting; play "male" sports like football, rugby or cricket; be referees or commentators of "male" sports: work in construction; or have positions as CEOs or executives of large companies, or as presidents or heads of state. If you find yourself defending why women can't or shouldn't do any job, it's time to reexamine your assumptions.

Some assumptions are so entrenched that they are regarded as fact, as the truth, and are often sacred cows – beyond criticism or even mild questioning. Here's one, "Human Resources (HR) exists to maximize employee performance in the service of an employer's strategic objectives." Really? Let's set aside the profoundly insulting and divisive title of "Human Resources." (If I were an alien wanting to harvest people to sell them to other aliens – either as food or as slaves, I don't care – I would have a Human Resources department.) The assumption that you need to maximize employee performance is fatally flawed in today's world of work. As we'll see later, the definition of an employee has become so broad that it is becoming meaningless. The understanding of "performance" has also changed dramatically – for instance, some people pay people to make as many mistakes as possible. And what is this "maximize" thinking? Optimize, yes, but the real issue is the assumption that people need an external party to "maximize" their performance. You'll also find many business thinkers who believe that the "maximize" mindset causes more problems than it solves because it means to make something or someone as large/fast/efficient/profitable/(pick a business performance metric) as possible – usually, to the exclusion of something else. Optimizing is about making the best or most effective use of something or someone.

WHAT IS WORK?

This is a fundamental question that often escapes examination because the answer is self-evident: "Work is what you do to make a living." That's what someone might say from their own perspective, but what about employers' views, or a union perspective. All of these views may be wrong in the modern workplace.

So, let's go back to first principles: Work is a physical or mental activity, carried out to achieve a result. This is such a broad definition that it includes sport, hobbies, reading, listening to music, and making love, most of which come under the heading of "leisure," which is explicitly the time when one is not working.

"Work" is also a place you go to, or a period of time (I'll see you after work.), a task (Did you get the work done?), and an exhortation (Work the problem!). It is also a social commentary (All work and no play.), and is used to control children (You can play after you finish your work.), and to praise people (She does good work.).

So, perhaps "work" is a more elusive concept than we thought. How about "employment" or "job?" We'll find that we can go down semantic rabbit holes for a long time and still not be satisfied with the answers. So we won't do that. However, the business environment understands what we mean when we talk about the workplace and workers, and a workforce, and working conditions, so there must be some way to exclude "non-work" like sport, leisure, listening to music, partying, and so on. It comes down to what people will pay for. This mercenary definition is probably our best bet at defining work in the modern environment. It includes employment, entrepreneurship, self-employment, and professional sport. It also provides for the concept of future payment – so you can be working on a business idea and no-one will mistake it for leisure. The definition is still imperfect, but at least it gives us a handle to advance the discussion on why the new world of work challenges the C-Suite.

Why will you pay for something? To achieve an outcome. The simple equation is: I pay, work happens, a result is achieved. A savvy entrepreneur will factor the business development time and work into his or her pricing so that they are paid for their work in retrospect.

In a digital world, work is often automated, but we pay for this automation. The automation is often hidden, so we have lost sight of it, but in the end, we are paying for it. A simple example is the spell-checker in my word processing package. I know it's there because it has just automatically corrected this sentence as I typed it. What I really typed was: "I know it's there becasue it has just automaticallt corrected…" The spell-checker, bless it, corrected my habitual finger coordination without me even knowing about it. But I paid for it when I bought the application, and I would not buy a word-processing app that did not have this feature. In fact, because I write so much, I have paid extra for a spell-checker on steroids – it checks spelling, context, grammar, punctuation, sentence structure, style, and vocabulary, among other things. So now I have paid for my original spell-checker, but I am not using it because I paid again for a better spell-checker.

What are people paying for explicitly now that they did not pay for in the past? Because of digitization and automation, much drudge-work is being done by machines. Computers and robots are cheaper, more consistent and reliable, handle repetitive, dull, or dangerous work, work through the night, don't take holidays or sick leave, and can be replaced or removed without anyone getting upset about it. If you're a businessperson, what's not to like? And if you're a Luddite, opposed to technology, what alternatives can you offer other than moral and ethical ones, which, unfortunately, will always fail against the profit motive? Computers and machines tend to replace two types of workers – low-level non-skilled workers like cleaners, machine attendants, tellers – anywhere the work is repetitive and not particularly complicated. The latest computers are replacing mid-level workers as AI (artificial intelligence) and RPA (Robotic Process Automation) are taking over processes that require uncomplicated decisions and repetitive activities. Perhaps when we ask ourselves: "What is work?" we are really asking: "What can and should people do, that others are prepared to pay for?"

Executives should be prepared to pay for activities and capabilities that machines cannot do – they should pay people to make decisions, be creative, use intuition, understand analog data (like pictures), and have insights. We should also be paying for soft skills like empathy, understanding, motivation, counseling, and – would you believe – touching. Being touched is a fundamental human need, but we have legislated touch out of the work and other environments. In a touch-phobic society, some people will pay to be touched – not inappropriately, though there are those people too – to be hugged or massaged. Studies have also shown that waiters, librarians, salespeople, advisors, and anyone who deals in a one-to-one relationship can improve the outcomes of simple interactions by including touch in the transaction. A machine can't do that.

WHY DO PEOPLE WORK?

This may seem to be as simple a question as: "What is work?" And in some ways it is, but in other ways, the problem has launched careers and theories that have lasted for years. The simple answer to the question is that people work to make a living so that they can buy food, accommodation, support their family, and afford their leisure activities. This touches on Maslow's hierarchy of needs which proposes that people need, in order of importance: Physiological needs (food, water, shelter, sleep), security (personal, emotional, health, and financial), belonging (friends and family), self-esteem, self-actualization, and transcendence. We won't go into detail here or consider the many academic criticisms of Maslow's hierarchy, but we can say that people work to meet their needs.

The issue of how you motivate people to work better, harder, and smarter, comes at the "why people work" question from an employer's perspective. It is this aspect that has made people's careers and fortunes. (After all, individuals won't pay you to tell them why they work, but organizations will pay you to tell them what motivates people to work.)

In 1911, Frederick Taylor introduced the concept of scientific management and sought to increase industrial efficiency through enforced standardization, enforced cooperation, and strict division of duties. He said that the manager's job was to do the enforcing. Taylor introduced time and motion studies, and, in short, revolutionized management. He also introduced the concept of pay for tasks, rather than pay for time. His famous, and often criticized, experiment with a worker named Schmidt at Bethlehem Steel showed that a man could be made to move 47 tons of pig-iron in a day rather than 12.5 tons, just by paying him per ton, rather than paying for a day's work. (The fact that the dollars per ton rate was much lower than the daily rate was a benefit to both workers and managers – or so Taylor asserted.)

In the 1920s, the concept of "participative management" was introduced, then lost, then revived again in the 1990s. The idea is simple: If people have a say in something and can influence outcomes, they tend to support it and strive for its success. We'll see later in this chapter how self-management is the cornerstone of a new type of organization that is starting to capture the attention of workers and managers, although in different ways.

In the 1950s, Douglas McGregor introduced Theory X and Theory Y workers – Theory X workers were lazy and unmotivated, while Theory Y workers were ambitious, energetic, and had self-control. The two categories were designed to help managers decide on the style they would adopt when managing people: Theory X workers should be closely supervised, be rewarded "externally" – with money and perks – and should be penalized when performance was lacking. Theory Y workers should be encouraged to work unsupervised to achieve internal job satisfaction.

There have been numerous "revolutionary" theories on what motivates people to work that have made their proponents rich and famous, and good for them. To summarize and analyze them would be fun but doesn't serve the purposes of this chapter, which is to outline the challenges that the new world of work presents to the C-Suite. For executives to understand why people work now, and what motivates people to work, they could consider the following list and apply it to their employees. Each employee will not have the same motivators, so regard this list as a menu of motivators, rather than a prescription for motivated people.

- People are motivated by money – insofar as it is tradable for the things that allow them to meet their needs. Economic theory does, however, show that "satisficing" is where people are satisfied with their pay and sets a limit on the motivation that money has on most people. Some people are, of course, never satisfied, but they are in the minority.
- People are also motivated by being kept engaged (actively supporting the outcome) and interested (actively applying thought). People like to be challenged and want to have the satisfaction of seeing a result. This is important for repetitive work – where someone gets a half-completed input, does something to it, and hands it on to someone else to complete. They do need to see the finished result.
- Most people are motivated by having autonomy and having discretion – allowing people to decide what they need to do to achieve the desired results, and also allowing them to choose how they will do the work. We'll see later that this motivator is the cornerstone of a new type of organization.
- Some people work to achieve mastery and expertise. This is particularly true of researchers, product developers, and computer system developers, but it can be true of salespeople, factory workers, drivers, and delivery clerks. These are the people to watch, as they are likely to become the managers and leaders of the future.

- Some people work for social engagement. They like people and like being with people – again, these are valuable people to have. Automation, AI, and RPA, or working from home or coffee shops do not provide the social interactions that people need to feel engaged in their work.
- Some people work for meaning. These are often teachers, nurses, volunteer workers, social workers, politicians – people who work for the greater good and what it means for society.

In 2013, Gallup conducted an extensive survey of workers that showed that only 13% were engaged by their work. Being engaged means that people perform as well as they can, support their organization's goals and values, and want to contribute to its success, while at the same time have a sense of their own self-worth. What has alarmed managers is that 87% of people are not engaged (they just pitch up, do their work, and go home), or are actively disengaged (they are negative, unhappy, and unproductive). If this sounds like the Theory X, Theory Y rerun, it is. Only it's from the other side – the implication is that managers have to change people – engage them – instead of managing them as they are.

The motivation of staff will remain on the agenda for managers, executives, and leaders for a long while, and probably rightly so. But as we will see, fewer people are prepared to work for one organization and prefer to provide services to multiple organizations at the same time – they are self-motivated. We will also see that this self-motivation can be incorporated into large organizations in surprising (and indeed productive and profitable) ways.

WHO WORKS?

This will be a short section. We'll stick to our provisional definition of work being what people do for pay, even though the description of work is much broader.

There is a traditional employer/employee work relationship. The employer works, of course, as does the employee. However, the definition of an employee is changing. We've discussed the disappearance of "jobs for life," so most people don't expect to be employed by the same organization forever, or even for more than a few years. There are temporary or part-time workers, interim managers, and gig workers. All of these do not expect to spend their whole day working for a single employer, or if they do, the timeframe for the job is measured in weeks or months. Another form of work is service or outsource work. Many, if not most, organizations use services or outsource some functions such as cleaning, security, catering, computer, transport, payroll … the list is pretty much as long as you like it. If an organization does not consider the function to be core, they will be able to find an external service provider to do it for them. This complicates the working environment: Some service-provider staff may have been working at the company longer and know more about it than full-time staff.

Millennials have been called "gig" workers or free agent workers. Over one third do not expect to work for an organization permanently. Instead, they expect piecework – a specific task or undertaking that has a set deadline, for which payment is made on completion. They work for several organizations, often at the same time. They want interesting projects and the opportunity to grow horizontally – within their current rank. A way of looking at it is that they wish to have their CVs to be strengthened by the work they do for you. They use their own technology but may expect assistance from mentors or even RPA – programs that remove the mundane tasks from their work, thus keeping it interesting. They are accustomed to finding information quickly and efficiently and expect to have access to the organization's information databases. They may expect some AI help here. Millennials work to live, not the other way around. They don't expect jobs for life, nor do they expect to be involved in non-work activities at the workplace.

Probably the most exciting development in answer to the question: "Who works?" is that teams work. And self-managed teams work even better. We'll cover the self-managed team concept at the end of this chapter.

WHERE AND WHEN DOES WORK HAPPEN?

The workplace itself is changing. Collaboration has become the norm for most workers, and they work better in groups – so fixed office space is less important to them as collaborative areas, project rooms, discussion areas, and hot-desking. The workspace is becoming less formal and more fluid. A recent study[1] showed that open-plan workspaces decreases productivity, decreases face-to-face interactions, and decreases creativity. The researchers ascribe this change in behavior to people feeling they were "on display," which increased their stress and decreased their psychological privacy – two factors which contributed to reduced creativity. If collaboration and creativity are reduced by open-plan offices, the new workspace should probably be organized around hubs – places where people working on the same project can congregate and share ideas. Open-plan workspaces have higher noise levels and more distractions, while "concentration hubs" should be quiet, focused areas.

Work times are also under the spotlight. In many countries, workers who have been with an employer for a few months are allowed to ask for flexible work times that suit them. Most workers tend to operate with flexible working times anyway – they work from home or over the weekend. Some workers plan their workday to avoid rush hour commuting, others to avoid commuting at all – 50% of workers work at least half the week from a location which is not the office, and it is axiomatic that the times that they work may differ from office hours. It is estimated that the USA could experience a $4.5 trillion boost to its economy annually as a result of flexible working.[2]

Workers define workplace flexibility as consisting of three elements: Time, place, and independence to select what work gets done when. The flexibility of work time and place is seen to improve diversity in the workplace, as women, pensioners, and people with health issues benefit from choosing their mode of work and from being able to balance their work-life priorities. Employers also cite flexibility as being a critical factor that job seekers expect to be met when looking for a job. Getting the right people is fundamental to improving organizational capabilities, so flexibility should be considered as a necessary condition of employment. However, flexibility places some responsibilities on the employer. Staff must be able to work flexibly. This means they must have the technology – there needs to be secure access to the organization's systems, access to secure printers and scanners, and collaboration systems need to be put in place to allow teams to work together wherever they are. The effort in providing flexible working environments is worth it, as 85% of businesses report that they are more productive, and 65% are more agile, as a result. Remote working is essential for a modern organization as half the workforce expects to work from somewhere other than the official office – whether it be from home, business lounges, client offices, or even coffee shops. While 75% of workers consider flexible working to be normal, only 62% of organizations have flexible work policies, and only 25% of these help their staff financially in setting up home offices

Additionally, flexible work allows organizations to reduce Capex (Capital Expenditure) and to consolidate their office spaces and locations. One of the reported challenges to introducing flexible work is said to be the attitude of the executive team – they don't understand the benefits, or worry that the culture will be affected, or some even believe that if people are not supervised closely, productivity will fall. The last supervision issue is false, and as one of the authors of the study into open-plan workspaces said:

> We assume that when we can see something, we understand it better. In this particular environment, and perhaps many others, what managers were seeing wasn't real. It was a show being put on for an audience. When the audience was gone, the real show went on, and that show was more productive.

The way that people think about work has changed. It is no longer a "place," neither does one spend eight hours a day at it. People regard innovation as an essential element of how they think about work and expect their ideas to be considered by decision-makers. They may have these ideas after hours, on weekends or while on holiday, and they expect to be able to interact with their organization at any time from any location so they can record their ideas, update their thinking, or test their ideas with colleagues. People also expect to be consulted on decisions that affect them – particularly on the technology that they use. And in 61% of cases, technology is imposed on staff without their involvement in the decision. We need a more inclusive approach to deciding which technologies our staff use. One CIO set up a portal where people rated various laptops. Over a short period, the IT department excluded themselves from laptop decisions, because when someone wanted a new laptop, they visited the portal and chose the highest-rated device. The portal expanded to other devices and software, particularly personal productivity applications like collaboration tools and project management applications. The IT department was seen as helpful to workers and lost its nickname: "The abominable no-men."

Job skills are also changing. More workers are taking "micro-courses" of one to three months to address a skills shortfall they believe that they have but need to do their work well. A portal approach will work here too. People rank the most useful courses they take, and other workers make informed decisions on the training they want to pursue.

Consequently, organizations should encourage their workers to upskill themselves in their choice of training continually, and so improve the overall capabilities of the organization. While the capability may remain constant, the level to which people can execute that capability changes, and it is this level that continuous training addresses. Another factor related to the skills that people possess is that formal qualifications, taking two to three years to acquire, are becoming less relevant to getting work done than micro-skilling. Extended qualification training programs necessarily cover areas and subjects that are not relevant to the job at hand and, importantly, do not interest the worker. Remembering that millennials look for interesting work, the same applies to their training. It must engage them or they won't complete it.

Social skills have also become crucial in the new world of work. Because collaboration is how work is done in the workplace and change and ambiguity dominate activities, the ability to communicate and to accommodate change are necessary skills, especially for leaders. Gardner identified nine types of intelligence, of which interpersonal intelligence is essential, and intrapersonal intelligence (understanding oneself) is indispensable to manage others and advance through the organizational hierarchy. Linguistic skills assist not only in interpersonal communication but also in conveying complex concepts. The ability to visualize mental models and have others understand them (spatial intelligence) helps people who work in groups or who are leaders. In school, we are taught mostly logical and linguistic skills, so it is useful to have micro-courses available for people who want to develop their other forms of intelligence. Other soft skills such as assertiveness, ethics, professionalism, expectation management, listening, and leadership are also available as short courses.

Another thing about learning is that it is closely linked to creativity. The creative process usually requires experimentation and then learning from the results. Ask any creative person and they'll tell you that they have made more mistakes than had successes. Many business systems don't allow for errors, and in some activities this is an appropriate culture. But where creativity is required, mistakes and learning must be accommodated. One approach is taken from the agile technique of building MVPs (Minimum Viable Products). These are working solutions that fulfill the minimum requirements of customers or the user to be useful to them. The MVP process is an experimentation and learning activity. There is the concept of being able to "pivot" at short notice. At a checkpoint, a decision is made to stop, continue, increase, or move in a different direction. These are not mistakes. Instead, they are pivot points. The term removes the stigma associated with errors and instead sees every checkpoint as a learning step. However, it is not only the activity that must be able to pivot – how we finance this experimentation and learning, how we change processes, and how decisions are made must all be incremental and able to pivot. Most crucial to this way of working is the ability to make decisions quickly and to delegate decisions to those most qualified to make them.

THE NEXT-GENERATION ORGANIZATION

Throughout this chapter, I've alluded to other ways of working, such as self-managed teams. However, self-managed teams are a small, but essential part of what Frederic Laloux,[3] calls "Evolutionary or Teal organizations," in his remarkable book "Reinventing Organizations." If you are interested in reinventing your organization, I urge you to read it. But we are concerned with evolving digitally savvy executives, so I'll give you the short version of what an Evolutionary Organization is.

Laloux traces the evolution of organizations from antiquity to present-day forms, which he describes as those that value replicable processes, hierarchies, innovation, accountability, and reward achievements. This sounds perfectly normal, but Laloux points to two things that make them less than satisfactory: In most people's inner being, they know there has to be a better way of doing things. Laloux believes that most, if not all people, have to wear a "mask" at work because they can't express emotion, intuition, or spirituality without enduring criticism or disapproval. Yet, everyone is emotional, intuitive, and spiritual. And if work is a place where you have to wear a mask, then it cannot be a whole and healthy place – and given that you often spend more time there than at home … well then. The second thing that makes current organizations "broken" models is that the replicable process, hierarchy, … values that were stated above are designed for different times and conditions than the present. For example, a hierarchy is a slow, inefficient, costly, and stressful way of dealing with complexity. Laloux makes many other points about how current organizational forms are sub-optimal and unsustainable, and found at least 12 organizations that do things so totally differently that most people label them as unworkable. Yet, they work, and have worked for years, and perform better than their competitors by a long way. (Interestingly, none of these organizations, according to Laloux, ever talks about competition – they just talk about doing what they do to the best of their ability. The CEO of one organization even coaches his "competitors" on how they can be better at what they do.)

There are three components of Evolutionary (or Teal) organizations identified by Laloux, and here I'll quote him directly:

- **"Self-management:** Teal organizations have found the key to upgrading their structures from hierarchical, bureaucratic pyramids, to powerful and fluid systems of distributed authority and collective intelligence.
- **Wholeness:** Organizations have always been places that encourage people to show up with a narrow "professional" self. Teal organizations have developed a consistent set of practices that invite us to drop the mask, reclaim our inner wholeness, and bring all of who we are to work.
- **Evolutionary purpose:** Teal organizations are seen as having a life and a sense of direction of their own. Instead of trying to predict and control the future, members of the organization are invited to listen and understand what the organization is drawn to become, where it naturally wants to go."

At a quick read, this might sound a little new-age, but on reading the book, I found the thinking grounded in reliable case studies. The main decisive factor though is that organizations that have implemented the above practices are thriving, growing, and, above all, happy places to work, and who can argue against that?

The way people work and want to work is usually not the way traditionally-minded executives work and want their people to work. But here's the thing. There is a groundswell of successful organizations and individuals that are demonstrating that a new way of working is sustainable, profitable, and importantly, healthier for everyone concerned.

One of the things that strikes me about Teal organizations is that they use Information Technology to communicate, collaborate, make decisions, and dismantle bureaucracy. Yet, all of them value, promote, and insist on time with people. This time is to be spent on people – how they feel, what they think, where they are going, and who they are. It is about creating an environment where people feel safe enough to be creative, express their doubts and concerns, and feel unique. When they do that they feel engaged, and in a world where 87% of people are not engaged at work, that has to be a good thing.

NOTES

1   Ethan S Bernstein and Stephen Turban, *The Impact of the "Open" Workspace on Human Collaboration*, Philosophical Transactions of the Royal Society B, 2018. https://royalsocietypublishing.org/doi/full/10.1098/rstb.2017.0239, [Accessed July 2019].
2   *The IWG Global Workspace Survey, IWG Jersey*, March 2019. www.iwgplc.com/global-workspace-survey-2019, [Accessed July 2019].
3   Frederic Laloux, *Reinventing Organizations: A Guide to Creating Organizations Inspired by the Next Stage of Human Consciousness*, Nelson Parker, Mills, MA, 2014.

CHAPTER SEVEN

Organizational change, pressure, and speed

Rather than discuss information technology, as we did in Chapter 5, I'd like to look at how digitization has changed the world, for the better and for the worse.

TECHNOLOGY AND THE ECONOMY

Information tech companies have overtaken the oil and gas companies to become the largest public companies in the world. Their revenue has grown from 0.5% of world GDP (gross domestic product) in 1992, to 1% in 2004, and is anticipated to reach 4% in 2026 and 8% in 2038. Interestingly, it is expected that a significant portion of this future growth will come from tech products that don't exist yet.[1] And estimates are that most of this new tech will come from start-ups that also don't exist yet, which is why the large tech companies are going out of their way to develop reciprocal relationships with start-ups by providing platforms and infrastructure on which they can build their solutions.

The pace of technological change is increasing in two ways: The creation of new technology and the adoption of new technology. Most people are aware of Moore's Law, which is loosely defined as information technology circuitry that fits into a given space doubles every 24 months, implying that the cost of information technology halves every two years. Moore himself never went this far, but his law has held true for decades and is regarded as axiomatic. The pace of change for non-IT technologies is also increasing. Swanson's law covers photovoltaic cells decreasing in cost, and the cost of sequencing the human genome (DNA) is falling faster than Moore's Law. Transportation, robotics, energy storage and generation, lighting efficiency, and financial services are all increasing their change rates, but it's worth keeping in mind that all of these non-IT technologies are improving on the back of IT improvements. Kartik Garda[2] observed that most disruptions are not in new technologies, but in older technologies where a threshold has been crossed. The threshold is usually in another industry – for example, exponential lighting efficiency and energy usage improvements through LEDs (Light Emitting Diodes) was possible only when diodes became available. Watch out for the next generation of LEDs – PLEDs (Perovskite LEDs), which, in four years of development, have matched the efficiency of the best LEDs, and two-way LEDs that can detect and absorb light as well as emit light.

Artificial Intelligence (AI) is another technology that had to wait for big data techniques amongst others. AI is on the threshold of becoming one of the most dramatic world-changing developments – mainly because of its impact on jobs and tax (governments can't tax AI productivity, and if they try, the AI can move to another country instantly, or indeed be spread across many countries – tax laws will never catch up). An industry as traditional as construction is about to undergo a catastrophic disruption because of robotics and 3D printing: It is probable that by 2025 buildings will be constructed in one-tenth of current times, at a similar cost reduction. This will also have an effect on real estate prices.

Technological deflation is a force that is affecting world economies dramatically, and for some reason, politicians and economists ignore it. The simple explanation is that, as explained above, many technologies (certainly the IT ones), halve their costs every two years. But it's a little more involved since the value of the technology that you buy also halves every 18 months. So your two-year-old phone which you purchased for say $400, can be sold at the same price as a brand new phone with more functions. This phenomenon means that from the day you open the package, your tech is worthless on the market. There is a small market for second-hand technology, of course, but it is minor when compared to vehicles and construction equipment – which are also technology, just not IT (yet).

Furthermore, technological deflation is accelerated by the combinatorial effect of technology. A smartphone is a camera, calculator, recorder, radio, storage medium, music player, geolocation device, and, of course, a phone. Interestingly, no smartphone advertisements try to sell the phone part of a smartphone. This combination of devices means that consumers are no longer buying five or six devices because one does the job – a further deflationary effect.

So here's the thing. Central banks try to keep deflation at bay through Quantitative Easing (QE). Deflation for an economy is a bad thing because it delays spending, which reduces demand, which decreases production, which causes job losses, which in turn leads to less spending, and so on, in a cycle that can ruin economies. But tech deflation is a good thing, providing the platform for innovation and start-ups (thus increasing jobs production and products). "Economic" deflation is at odds with "technological" deflation. QE has been in effect on a large scale since 2007, yet the world inflation rate has dropped from 8% to 2% in that period – remember that QE is designed to increase or at least steady the inflation rate. Only a minority of commentators suggest that tech deflation is the cause of the drop and will continue to be so into the future. They say that QE is here to stay and will become a feature of economies. But as Kartik Garda says: "No Western politician or central banker has ever uttered a single sentence about the accelerating rate of technological change and how policy has to mirror it in both agility and scope."

The rates of adoption of new technologies have increased and continue to grow as well. While telephones took 60 years for the adoption rate to reach 80%, mobile phones took only 10 years, and smartphones 5 years. Also increasing is the rate of acceptance of social norms. The recognition of same-sex marriages was incredibly quick, while inter-racial marriage took hundreds of years to gain acceptance. These are not relative comparisons, except to say that social issues today are debated worldwide, and opinions and drives to change are relatively instantaneous today, and politicians, if they are wise, can track the mood with ease and make amendments to legislation accordingly. All of this is, of course, dependent on, and facilitated by, IT. Information tech has become widely used in electoral campaigns to influence public opinion and primarily to involve young people in political life.

The economy is deeply affected by IT, over and above the deflationary effects of technology. Not only are economies affected faster by trends, bubbles, and rumors, but the foundations of economic thinking are having to change. Adam Smith, regarded as the pioneer of political-economic thought, advanced two theories which are still held to be relevant, even though the digital economy proves them to be false. He proposed that in a free-market economy, the rules of supply and demand define how prices are set. Demand occurs when there is a scarce commodity and the suppliers of such products are often able to determine the price they want to be paid. He also proposed his theory of absolute advantage, where he said that if an individual, company or country can produce a greater quantity of a product or service than their competitors, using the same amount of resources, they have the absolute advantage. In a digital economy, both supply and demand, and absolute advantage are on shaky ground.

As far as IT is concerned, we have entered an economy of abundance. This does not mean everything is free, but that it is oversupplied, hence the price drops. Most manufacturers would keep their prices high even though their input costs are decreasing, but they can't do this because of oversupply, and they have to pass any of their cost-savings on to the consumer. Thanks to IT, abundance is experienced in many other areas – knowledge, training, entertainment, searching (jobs, housing, goods, services), publishing, books, and many others. Indeed, websites like Upwork, make the sourcing of experts to do a once-off job for you an auction for the lowest bidder. And due to exponential improvements, energy, transport, education, and, if you grow it yourself, food. Most experts agree that by 2030, most commonly-held scarce commodities will be in a state of abundance – which makes the economics of scarcity and supply and demand an outdated discipline. There are several proponents on "new economics," some of whom are strident ("The economy disadvantages everyone but the rich."), some are reasoned ("It doesn't make sense to think in industrial revolution terms, about the present and future."), and some are academic institutions ("How should we teach economics to the next generation of leaders?"). There is a growing recognition that current economic theory and the consequent political decisions just aren't serving the general population in a digital world.

A key concept to understand in interrogating the scarcity/abundance problem is that of rival and excludable goods and their converse, non-rival and non-excludable goods. A rival good is one where if I consume or use it, others cannot use it – food, clothing, laptops. Non-rival goods – sunlight, air – can be consumed without denying consumption by others. Rivalry is a physical property. However, excludable and non-excludable goods are legal concepts which concern ownership. This is my house, or any privately owned good or property is excludable.

Rival excludable goods are what markets are made for, and upon which, much past and present-day economic theory is based. Even in the pre-digital age, many distortions of these two dimensions occurred to benefit profits and protect ownership. Patents and intellectual property rights make non-rival goods into rival goods. With a patent, if I have an idea and register it, no-one else can have the idea, or use it without my permission. Intellectual property rights protect the investment that was made in developing concepts and material. On the surface, these legal instruments are logical, even if they had to be artificially created. In the digital world, the idea of a "commons" is not only gaining acceptance but is also global. The digital "commons" originates from a place of abundance, as well as from a moral perspective. If the producer of knowledge or an app is satisfied that he or she is receiving enough, then why should others not use and build on their work? In a digital commons, traditionally rival goods are made into non-rival goods.

The real tragedy relates to excludable and non-excludable goods. Fish, forests, minerals (indeed all of earth's resources) are non-excludable. The tragedy is that each consumer will try to use them before another consumer exhausts the supply. This leads to competitive depletion instead of cooperative conservation, which would be in the best interest of all parties. There are many international agreements on the use of non-excludable resources, which are often manifested in breaches of the agreement instead of conformance to it.

Absolute advantage has its roots in productivity, but Brynjolfsson and McAfee[3] show that while productivity continues to climb in the USA, jobs have been stagnating since 2000. Brynjolfsson says:

> Productivity is at record levels, innovation has never been faster, and yet at the same time, we have a falling median income, and we have

fewer jobs. People are falling behind because technology is advancing so fast, and our skills and organizations aren't keeping up.

So, absolute advantage may still be a valid theory, but jobs are at risk. But politicians and bankers don't seem to concern themselves with technological change and the impact it has on work and society – they certainly are tardy in introducing policies to address technological impacts.

The summary of all of the above is that past economic theories are breaking down and are seen to serve the few to the detriment of the many. And governments and economists (the few) are not doing anything about it. On the bright side, digitalization is accelerating the economic theory "crisis," while at the same time accelerating people's understanding of it and raising global resistance to current economic dogma. Kartik Garda observes that in an instant, connected, and globalized world, where an idea is obstructed and resisted, technology allows for the obstructers to be bypassed. Soon, one government will adopt a new economic theory, and the rest will follow. Those that are slow to adapt will experience a steeper disruption curve when they do.

TECHNOLOGY AND SOCIETY

The effect of digitization on society is both dramatic and subtle. It is dramatic because if we take the end-point and compare it to the pre-digitization society, we are amazed that people could even operate in those days. It is subtle, because digitization is pervasive throughout society, and it has been happening for a long time. Digitization is not an event that occurred once and then that was it. It has happened over 50 years in three waves, and the fourth wave is upon us. The first wave is regarded as mundane now but was a revolution and revelation at the time. This was simply called data processing – mainframes could process corporate and government information. Associated with this localized processing power was the development of networks and telecommunications – again, in those days, individual companies leased lines from telcos and ran their own systems. The second wave was both the development of PCs and the internet. This made computing personal while freeing up organizations from having to possess and run their own networks. This wave also initiated the practice of individuals dealing directly with organizations through the web and opened up many new trends that we may regard as "business as usual" today – online shopping, online travel bookings, online search and compare of goods (leading to the globalization of shopping), social networking, online celebrities, video streaming … the list goes on. The third wave involves advanced technologies such as AI, the Internet of Things (IoT), big data and analytics, and robotics. The fourth wave is often called the fourth industrial revolution (4IR) but is probably the fourth digital revolution as well. It is a merging of technologies that blurs the lines between the physical, digital, and biological spheres.

The social impacts of the first wave of digitization were generally positive. Data processing and networking allowed industries to scale (operate over a more comprehensive geography) and grow more rapidly. This led to a growth in employment, particularly in the service industries – financial, healthcare, education, and tourism. There was also a growth in household income (perhaps because it initiated the two-parent working family) and facilitated social inclusion by giving people access to information, government services, and leisure activities.

The second wave, with the internet and personalization of computing, allowed for distance education, remote work, e-commerce, and collaborative businesses – where several businesses cooperate in providing a single service or product. Innovation and start-ups became easier and more numerous, which led to a demand for labor in specific areas such as digital services, collaborative enterprise management, innovation, product development and design, and other areas that did not exist before. However, at the same time, repetitive and low-skilled jobs were automated and replaced. Service jobs and counseling and caring jobs remained safe from replacement. The internet had a generally positive effect on society, although some elements of society are slow to use the internet features and advantages effectively. Still to catch up are security and welfare, education, healthcare, and right at the end of the internet impacted "industries" is government. Not only are governments slow to adopt the tech enablers that their citizens use, but they are also glacially slow in formulating policy and regulation covering information technologies.

The third wave of digitization has significant implications for productivity improvement, without a concomitant increase in the number of jobs – in fact, the third wave bodes ill for jobs, while at the same time improving the delivery of social services through improved "sense and respond" processes using AI, IoT, and big data analytics. There is still a fair amount of speculation on the effect of the third wave of digitization on jobs, but it is generally agreed that those people who lose jobs will be unable to find work again unless they re-skill to a significant degree. And there is some doubt if this reskilling will be possible, given the history and aptitude of the people replaced by technology.

Therefore, governments and policy-setting bodies need to be more concerned about the third wave than previous waves. Much of the populist votes in recent years has been attributed to the reduction of jobs in the economy. While people often blame immigration, IT has undoubtedly reduced the number of jobs available in the marketplace, and AI and robotics will accelerate this trend. A 2013 analysis[4] estimated that 47% of US jobs were at risk from computerization. Of the 702 occupations analyzed, the most at risk were anticipated to be telemarketers, accountants and auditors, retail salespersons, technical writers, real estate sales agents, and commercial pilots. The least at risk were firefighters, editors, chemical engineers, the clergy, athletic trainers, dentists, and therapists. These occupations provide negotiation, persuasion, originality, and creativity, which (at the moment) AI cannot do. We can expect a reaction from people who suffer job losses once they realize the part AI and technology play in their situation.

TECHNOLOGY AND THE ENVIRONMENT

Many years ago I was talking to a CIO friend of mine. His company was a petroleum producer, and he said he was concerned about the ethics of his job. He said that technology helped his and other companies become more efficient and to move faster. The problem was that they were becoming more efficient at using non-renewable resources and using them faster. I suppose that is true of technology in many industries. Of course, technology also improves lives and provides jobs. So, the discussion becomes about the wise use of technology. And one thing capitalism has demonstrated, is that it's more about profit and consumption than about responsibility and wisdom.

Technology does have a positive effect on the environment, and it can be more positive going into the future. Smart cities and intelligent buildings are all about using energy and other resources more efficiently. The renewable energy industry is a no-brainer. The sharing economy, using online platforms to innovate and share resources, is equally beneficial to the environment. Companies like Blablacar which is a long-distance carpooling platform, or Turo – a peer-to-peer car rental service. There's Vinted, a used clothing online store and Engie, which shares resources across construction sites and provides for mini-grid electricity sharing. All of these have a profit motive but get that profit through sharing. IoT (sensing devices) reduces resources used in factories and in agriculture by anticipating shortfalls and by preventing the overuse of resources where they are sufficient. There's a weeding robot, which is set loose in fields and eliminates the need for herbicides. IoT is also used in smart parking, notifying drivers of parking spots and removing the need for driving around. Some waste companies use IoT to sense when waste bins are full and due for pickup, thus reducing their transport and fuel consumption. E-commerce optimizes logistics and transportation. Information flows freely, so spillage and pollution become visible immediately. PWC[5] released a report in 2018 in which they consider the game-changers that AI will bring to the environment. These include autonomous and connected electric vehicles, distributed energy grids, smart agriculture, weather forecasting, and climate modeling, disaster response, optimization of water resource management, and real-time environmental monitoring and response. Digitization can be good for the planet.

However, the adverse effects of the digital economy are, as stated before, the changes in production and consumption patterns. Furthermore, the digital ecosystem and the energy required to run it produces 2% of global emissions in data centers (this is a conservative estimate), which is equivalent to emissions from aviation. Also, the internet uses about 8% of energy in the UK,[6] and predictions are that by 2035 it could use all current UK power. Another issue is that the production of a single computer is resource-intensive: The UN has calculated that it takes 240kg of fossil fuels, 22kg of chemicals, and 1,500 liters of water to produce one computer. The energy required is nine times more to produce a computer than that device uses in its lifetime. Disposing of technology is also a major environmental problem with e-waste, or techno-trash, amounting to 5% of all solid waste. The little that is recycled (12.5% according to the EPA) is done poorly. Only 29% of e-waste is handled according to best practices. For example, Guiyu in China is a significant recycling destination. Hydrochloric acid is thrown on the items to expose the steel and copper to be recycled. High levels of lead poisoning are reported among Guiyu residents. Recycling e-waste is more profitable than mining the original ores. One ton of circuit boards is estimated to contain 40 to 800 times more gold than one metric ton of ore. There is 30 to 40 times more copper in a ton of circuit boards that can be mined from one metric ton of ore.

So, in summary, the digital ecosystem is good and bad for the world. It's the same old story – it's not what we do, it's how we do it. I'm not holding my breath, though.

COMPETITION, SPEED, AND IMPACT

John Hagel[7] says: "Technology has a dark side for business." It intensifies competition, it accelerates the pace of change, and it escalates local developments to have global impacts.

Digitalization comes in three forms – you digitalize products, processes, and people. And digital products also come in three forms. Firstly, you can have a purely digital product – books, apps, productivity tools, connectors, and so on are digital. Uber, Airbnb, Travelstart, and online banking are all digital products, supported by back-office functions. Then you have physical products which are enhanced by digital tech – motorcars, smartphones, home security, and the like all have a physical manifestation, but would be so much less without their digital components. Finally, you have digitally "wrapped" products. For instance, a mountain bike, which is a very physical product, can be wrapped in a digital site which is a virtual showroom, a trouble-shooting area, a maintenance tips area, and a cycling and fitness tips area. None of these is the bike, but they all make the bike experience more valuable to the customer. IT is more than an enabler of digital processes for products. So, technology indeed intensifies competition. You may have a great product, but if it does not have a digital component, you may not be competitive.

Technology also accelerates the pace of change. We've covered the life cycle of large organizations (one-third of what they were 40 years ago), but the product life cycle has also accelerated, as has the pace at which technology itself changes. The compressed product life cycle and accelerated technological change have consequences for business planning. Projects lasting longer than a year will find themselves in new territory when they reach their goal. If someone beat you to the product, it may be relatively mature with significant upgrades by the time you produce your product. That's why you should investigate the concept of MVPs (Minimum Viable Products). The product has the minimum features which will provide some desired functionality or features for a customer. Then you test the MVP with a few friendly customers. They give feedback and you either improve the product, take a different tack, or stop with the product altogether. The advantage is that your investment is contained. Business planning is also a problem. There is an axiom that the half-life of a benefit is six months. This means that in six months, half the benefits you envisaged your product or service providing customers will be unneeded. People change and their requirements change with them. So, your planning cycles should be in months, not years. This doesn't mean that you don't have a vision for five years or a goal that you are trying to reach, but these act a guide rail on your journey – your planning happens in much shorter cycles.

Hagel also said that technology escalates local developments to have global impacts. This means that the development of a new product (especially a digital one) can be released in California, and within months it may be affecting your business. This is because information is global and instant. Customers may ask why you don't provide that service, or they may merely change – especially if it's a digital product.

Nicholas Carr takes a different tack, worrying that technology makes us dependent, removes middle-level jobs, and robs us of initiative. Brynjolfsson suggests that organizations achieve "scale without mass." Whatever the argument, technology has changed the way business (and humanity) works. Competition, speed, connectedness, start-ups punching above their weight, and other technology-enabled forces will change the way large organizations operate. The C-Suite will need to think, lead, and act outside the box, with courage and decisiveness.

NOTES

1 Max Marmer, *A Look at How Technology Is Reshaping the Global Economy*, Medium, February 2018. https://medium.com/@maxmarmer/a-look-at-how-technology-is-reshaping-the-global-economy-c716c4681e06, [Accessed August 2019].
2 Kartik Garda, *The Accelerating TechnOnomic Medium (ATOM)*, 2016. https://atom.singularity2050.com/, [Accessed July 2019].
3 Erik Brynjolfsson and Andrew McAfee, *Jobs, Productivity and the Great Decoupling*, MIT, Cambridge, MASS, 2012. http://81.47.175.201/flagship/attachments/Jobs_Productivity_and_the_Great_Decoupling.pdf], [Accessed August 2019.
4 Carl Frey and Michael Osborne, *The Future of Employment: How Susceptible are Jobs to Computerisation?* September 2013. https://oxfordmartin.ox.ac.uk/downloads/academic/The_Future_of_Employment.pdf, [Accessed July 2019].
5 PWC, *Fourth Industrial Revolution for the Earth. Harnessing Artificial Intelligence for the Earth*, 2018. https://pwc.com/gx/en/sustainability/assets/ai-for-the-earth-jan-2018.pdf, [Accessed July 2019].
6 Andrew Ellis, The Net to Drain All Britian's Power, *The Times*, March 2015. https://thetimes.co.uk/article/net-to-drain-all-britains-power-prm2qx8czp0, [Accessed July 2019].
7 John Hagel, *Scaling Edges: How to Radically Transform Your Organization*, Idea Bite Press, 2014.

CHAPTER EIGHT

Function and process thinking are holding back your organization

The traditional functional paradigm has done more to impede customer-focused, business performance improvement over the past two decades than almost any other factor.[1]

(Andrew Spanyi – Business Process Management expert)

Functions and processes have helped executives design and improve their business operations since the 1920s. But while still useful, considering this to be the only way of looking at organizational activities, in the digital, instant, complex, and customer-driven environment, this approach is limiting at best, and destructive at worst.

Andrew Spanyi, a proponent and practitioner of enterprise business process management, believes that thinking along functional lines promotes silo thinking and turf protection, and an undue preoccupation with organizational structure. Furthermore, such thinking distorts performance measurement and executive rewards. We'll see later why I also believe that process thinking may have similar limiting effects on the organization.

FUNCTIONS IN ORGANIZATIONS

Functions are organizational units designed to deal with similar actions and processes – for example, marketing, operations, human resources, and so on. People with related skills and capabilities are assigned to the functions where these skills will be most useful. This is all logical and very, very industrial thinking – the "organization as a machine" if you like. The organization as a machine metaphor is prevalent and, of course, started in the industrial revolution. We've all heard people use words and phrases like: things are really humming, it's a well-oiled operation, re-engineering, firing on all cylinders, or I'm just a cog in the machine. These are all machine metaphors. If the organization is a machine, it can be designed to do exactly what we want it to do. Every component of a machine has a specific function which executes repetitively, without variation, giving us reliable overall performance.

Dee W Hock is a commentator on organizations and says on his home page[2]: "Why are organizations everywhere, whether political, commercial, or social, increasingly unable to manage their affairs?" And "Why are people, everywhere, increasingly in conflict with and alienated from the organizations of which they are part?" One answer he gives to his own questions is machine-based thinking where he says that everything (social, physical, biological) can be understood.

> ... as clock-like mechanisms composed of separable parts acting upon one another with precise, linear laws of cause and effect. ... if we could once understand the parts of something and the laws governing them, we could reconstruct the whole into a predictable, controllable mechanism operating in accordance with our desires. We have, for more than three centuries, worked diligently to organize society in accordance with that concept, believing that with ever more reductionist, scientific knowledge, ever more specialization, ever more technology, ever more efficiency, ever more linear education, ever more rules and regulations, ever more command-and-control management, we could engineer societal organizations in which we could issue commands at one place and get precise results at another, and know with certainly (sic) which commands to issue for which results. Never mind that human beings must be made to behave as cogs and wheels in the process.

He goes on to say that we ignore the fact that people and the world don't operate like a machine, and that the results and behaviors we get seldom support the machine metaphor. Finally, he says: "Over time, what we have gotten is all too obvious – obscene maldistribution of wealth and power, environmental devastation, and crumbling societies." Enough said, other than to agree with him and add my two-cents worth: I believe that if we don't stop thinking and acting the way we do, then humanity is a threatened species, and perhaps that's a good thing too. Heaven knows the rest of the species will breathe a sigh of relief when we've gone.

There are many metaphors for organizations, with Gareth Morgan[3] describing eight types. While we won't go into these here, two of Morgan's categories are aligned with the machine metaphor – the organization as an instrument of domination and as a psychic prison. These are harsh metaphors, but Morgan describes them respectively as metaphors for exploitation, control and unequal distribution of power, and for ways that organizations entrap their employees. Hierarchies are about control and distribution of power, and functions, while they do not necessarily entrap employees, they certainly place them in boxes and constrain what they can and cannot do.

Functions are designed by senior management and portrayed as organizational structures. One of the things that we often miss is that a chart of an organizational structure is both hierarchical (organized in levels) and columnar (organized in vertical lanes or silos). It is not merely about standardization and specialization, because power is also built into the structure. Who can make decisions is structured hierarchically and what they can decide about is organized in silos. There are very few organizations where these decisions are made participatively about who works where, what they can and should do, how they should do it, who makes decisions, and why they're doing it in the first place. Let's unpack that sentence a little. In the vast majority of organizations, people are allocated to departments and functions (who works where) and given job descriptions (what they can and should do). How they should do it is defined by procedures, standards, and policies. Who makes decisions are specified in the delegation of authority, and why they are doing it is laid out in the strategy, vision, mission, and goals. All these activities are usually decided and communicated by senior management. After all, they might say, it would be chaos if we allowed people to choose this stuff for themselves. There *are* organizations where all of these decisions and more are made by staff on the ground, but more about that later.

The point is that functions reinforce command and control, standardization and specialization, and power and the corresponding restraint of others' power. Command and control are a military concept, a developed antiquity. Commanders came from nobility and their authority was absolute and often brutal. Standardization is essential in machines and products because they allow components to be replaceable. And specialization is about the division of labor, with every person having a place and job – but the emphasis for me is on "division" and "labor." Division helps rulers (and managers) to control people and groups, often by setting themselves against each other, and labor implies that people simply perform activities that they are directed to do. And how many of us like to be called labor anyway?

There are alternatives to functions, organization charts, command and control, division of labor, and standardization and they are usually significantly more efficient and effective than traditional structures and methods. But they do come with their own problems.

The two main alternatives to hierarchical functions are self-managed teams and self-organizing systems. Frederic Laloux[4] went in search of the next generation organization and found a number that fitted his criteria. They all had common features, of which self-managed teams and self-organizing systems were two of the three essential elements of the next generation of organization. The third feature was something he called "wholeness in the workplace," but it is beyond the scope of this discussion (see Chapter 6, where I briefly describe Laloux's findings). He describes a home-nursing organization in the Netherlands, which has 800 self-managed teams of 10 to 12 people. There is no team leader and above the teams, no managers. For every 40 or 50 teams, there is a coach that teams can call to help them with any problem they encounter. They do have a head office, but it has only 28 people who mostly deal with the administration of the interface between other companies and governmental bodies and themselves. So here we have a company of 9,000 people with a small head-office, no managers, and one CEO (whose role is mostly to represent the company, and certainly not to manage it). Their success has been stellar, and many other companies are starting to implement their ideas.

PROCESSES IN ORGANIZATIONS

It started, of course with the industrial revolution, where a manufacturing process depended on, well, processes. A process is simplified as inputs converted into outputs. The primary manufacturing industry in the revolution comprised of textiles where raw cotton fiber was separated from its seed, baled, and sent to the factory. There, the cotton fibers were spun into yarn, which was then spun or woven into cloth, which was dyed, and then made into clothes. Each step had inputs, a conversion process, and an output. Simple enough. The industrial revolution mechanized these processes, for example, Eli Whitney's cotton gin could separate 50 pounds of cotton from its seed per day, where a single person (usually a slave) took ten hours to separate one pound. This multiplication of productivity occurred throughout the production process. Give a thought, however, to what we have lost: uniqueness, crafting, and the personal touch, and we have replaced muscle-power, a renewable form of energy, with machine-power, using non-renewable energy. There is no doubt that process thinking in a manufacturing environment is an essential element of designing and improving manufacturing operations. It is also the primary source of standardization versus difference, repeatability versus original, conformity versus diversity, specialization versus holism, and frankly, depersonalization versus humanity. I went to the bank this week which had sent two credit cards to different branches for me to collect – neither being the branch I had asked for. All they could say was that something had gone awry with the process – no responsibility in there at all. Which comes back to the organization as a machine: Engineers build machines and managers design processes. If something goes wrong, you can't blame the staff on the ground, and you can't talk to the manager concerned.

The dictionary definition of "process" is a systematic series of actions conducted to achieve some result. The words "systematic" and "series" are essential to our discussion of digitalization. Systematic suggests orderly, organized, and part of a system. But in the digital world, orderly and organized are less than satisfactory ways of describing how customers, suppliers, governments, and society interact with each other. The modern "system" of commerce is deeply complex, to the extent that it appears chaotic at times. (More about this later, where we deal with complex adaptive systems which were identified by scientists as the way that nature deals with apparent chaotic inputs and interactions.)

It is useful to think of these complex and chaotic interactions as a network of non-linear links and transactions. And that's where a process view of the world breaks down. Transactions and communications are not linear or systematic; neither are they orderly nor organized. Information flows freely and in many directions at once. Interactions happen at the core of the organization and at the edge. Indeed, interactions often occur outside the organization, which has little knowledge of them but is affected by them. In many cases, transactions occur without human action or experience of them.

This is not to say that process thinking is unhelpful. It is an essential element of an executive's toolkit. Critically, the executive should not believe that this is the only way to view organizational interactions. Complexity and non-linearity are not well represented by process thinking, even though the components of complex, non-linear interactions may be. Non-linear processes are not sequential or straightforward. There are no straight lines (and process mapping is all about straight lines). Examples of non-linear thought are logarithmic or inverse relationships. When internet commerce became widely used, many sales grew in a non-linear way – you didn't have to sell to one person. Instead, many people from anywhere in the world could buy your product.

Another example of non-linear behavior is the customer journey in your organization. I recently saw a customer journey map of a customer buying shoes online. Throughout the journey, the customer referenced the e-shop three times and interacted with between one and six different departments at any stage of her journey. In the 31 touchpoints with the company, she interacted with the customer services department 23 times, and there wasn't one department that didn't interact with her at least three times. This is hard, if not impossible, to represent or even think about, in a process way. Complex mapping, or even three-dimensional mapping, is needed if we are to understand non-linear interactions.

There are alternatives to functional and process thinking. An answer lies in both self-managed teams and in self-organizing systems.

SELF-MANAGED TEAMS

A self-managed team takes collective responsibility for ensuring that the team operates effectively and meets its targets. They work within a broad framework of aims and objectives to reach a common goal. These aims and objectives are usually arrived at through consultation and conversation with other teams. In general, these teams have considerable autonomy over what work they do and how they will do it. They share decision-making and problem-solving and manage internal performance issues themselves. Most self-managed teams have their own budgets, and in many cases can purchase equipment or the tools they need to achieve their targets without recourse to a central financial function, except for advice and guidance. In most cases, they set their own performance criteria, and in some cases, even set their own salaries. Because they have autonomy over how they will get work done, they can use their full skill-set and train themselves up to do a job that the team needs doing. If they do have a team leader, his or her job is to support them, sort out problems with other units, and act as a representative. If this sounds like a recipe for chaos, poor performance, and wasteful spending, keep in mind that all self-managed teams work within a strict set of guidelines and are driven to achieve an overarching goal (which they usually set collaboratively with the rest of the organization). There is nothing tougher than working in an environment where you have a say in goals and objectives and are deemed successful or not by your colleagues.

There are several benefits to having self-managed teams, not the least being the opposite of everything that hierarchical functions impose on them: They decide which team they want to work in, define their own, often fluid, job descriptions, and how they will get the work done. They make or contribute to decisions, especially those that will affect them, and they contribute to the strategy conversation. Needless to say, individual motivation is high, productivity is improved, and commitment to the organization is often intense. There are cost savings because there's no hierarchy to support, no duplication of activities, indirect labor costs (e.g. purchasing, quality management, materials handling, accounting, HR), and, of course, productivity is increased. It has been found that because decision-making is distributed, the organization is more flexible and responsive to customer needs, and customer satisfaction is higher. Because teams decide how they will work, innovation and operational improvements are significantly higher than in hierarchical structures. What's not to like?

There are some problems with self-managed teams, usually associated with the set-up period. If the culture of the organization has been one of command and control, managers and even staff will find it challenging to adopt new, freer practices. Team members may initially shun extra responsibilities, and managers and supervisors will resist having responsibilities (and power) taken away from them. Everyone will need training and coaching in how self-managed teams work and will probably need training in the extra responsibilities that they take on, for instance, all the indirect labor activities they will now perform themselves. While this sounds like "management" saying, "we're not doing this stuff anymore, you do it," do remember that there will be no managers in the future, so funds will be available to make teams larger if needed. Generally, it is found that teams stay the same size, but overtime pay may go up for a while until productivity catches up.

Communication is sometimes a problem with self-managed team organizations, but here technology comes to the rescue. Within the team, communication is usually verbal, or a team conversation site is set up. The organization can also set up cross-team platforms and company-wide platforms for discussions on more general topics. One of the critical success factors is the communication system, so this is not to be taken lightly. Luckily, since there are not so many collaborative and project management tools, discussion boards, and newsrooms available this is relatively quickly resolved. One of the biggest problems for self-managed teams is power (and the loss of it) of executives and managers, and I believe it to be the primary reason why so few organizations have set them up. Sad really.

There is one final form of a self-organizing team that is worth a mention – these are called communities of practice (CoPs). A CoP is a group of people who share a craft, profession or interest. They may be in the same organization or not. For instance, there may be a financial CoP for a group of self-managed teams, where people share information and techniques relevant to that organization. Alternatively, there may be a finance CoP for all self-managed teams across organizations – this is usually called a community of interest. CoPs sometimes evolve naturally or can be deliberately created, but if they are deliberately created, they should be designed so that they can (and should) change once they have been set up. In an organization with self-managed teams, the deliberate creation of CoPs adds to the communication and learning tools, so it should not be ignored. Community membership is often determined by the knowledge of the members but may be defined by the activity, profession or interests of a member. Members can be active or passive.

SELF-ORGANIZING SYSTEMS

Self-organization is a natural and universal process (except in most organizations). It is a process where some form of order arises from interactions between parts of a system. A system is a group of interacting components, often with a temporal or spatial boundary. The self-organizing process does not need external control but does require an initial trigger. Feedback loops are essential to self-organization. The system is usually robust and able to self-correct and self-repair even in the most difficult of circumstances.

That's the theory. Now let's talk about self-organizing systems in an enterprise context. I came across a paper which defined over 20 components of self-organizing systems, but in an earlier book,[5] I developed an approach to self-organization that will work in organizations.

Self-organizing systems are part of a scientific discipline of complex adaptive systems. There is a difference between complicated and complex.

Complicated systems have many components, but each system works exactly the same way over time. Complex systems react differently every time. They seem to be thinking, learning systems that change to meet new conditions. Complex adaptive systems are "complex," because they exhibit many independent interactions, "adaptive" because they respond to their environment, and "systems" as the components and interactions are linked.

Business is a complex adaptive system, not a complicated linear one, which is why it cannot be managed linearly, with linear processes and hierarchies of functions and roles. Employees interact with each other and the environment and adapt to changing conditions. At first sight, it would seem that you need complex procedures to manage complex adaptive systems. However, scientists have found that a few simple rules which govern the behavior of individual components of the system tend to generate complex systems.

In 1987, scientist Craig Reynolds[6] modeled the behavior of a flock of birds, wheeling, diving, and swooping in unison. Reynolds developed a computer simulation that replicated the action of the flock by giving each "bird" three rules to obey: (1) fly in the direction of other birds; (2) try to match the velocity of neighboring birds; (3) avoid bumping into things. After a short while, the "birds," having been randomly placed in space, had "formed" themselves into a "flock" that behaved in a very similar way to real flocks of birds – a self-organizing system.

A lesson for business is that if people and teams have a few simple rules and guidance, they will tend to organize themselves to get the work done. The first prerequisites for complex adaptive business systems are to recognize that business is just such a system. Complex systems are managed by "distributed control" rather than "central control." This spells the end of command-and-control and insists on more human, personal relationships.

The essential elements of self-organizing systems are:

- A driving sense of purpose that binds all system components – Laloux calls this the evolutionary purpose.
- A few rules (three or four only).

- Units which can act within the purpose, obeying the rules.
- Constant attention to the environment in which the system operates.

The job of executives is to create the driving sense of purpose in the organization, monitor that purpose, and help the organization to adjust when the purpose needs adjustment. But they need to let everybody follow that direction on their own. In some instances, where organizations have self-managed teams, the evolution of the driving purpose is left to the people in the organization. Laloux describes a company where one team identified a new service that the company could provide. They started providing that service themselves, independently. They set up the support structures and personnel for the service and just started doing it. When one of the team members talked to the CEO about this new service and asked whether it should be rolled out throughout the company, he said: "Why don't you put the service, what you've done, and how you've done it on to the discussion portal and see what people say?" Other teams adopted the services, made improvements, and soon the entire company was offering the new service. There was no management direction, interference or top-down command. The company had developed a new element of their services, which became part of their driving purpose.

A few axioms need to be defined. An axiom is a principle that is held to be true and needs no proof. (I dislike the word "rule" because that's heading in the direction of command and control.) Here leadership is important. In complexity science, there is a concept of fractals. A fractal is the smallest part of a system, which, when multiplied by itself, develops into complex systems. The management fractal question is this: What rule or rules if multiplied throughout the organization will result in self-organizing behavior that serves the purpose of the organization? An example that comes to mind in a self-managed organization that I worked with is that every team had a profit and loss statement. That doesn't sound too radical, but when combined with their two other fractal axioms of consulting and sharing, some very powerful teamwork emerged. Because one person knew he was no good at sales, he would enlist the support of the others to find leads for him. He would, of course "pay" them for their leads. By the same token, people would often outsource work that they could not do or would need a team to do, and they would have to set up and "pay" a project team. Finally, a person could "sell" research services to the others if she so chose. The profit and loss statement encapsulated the payroll, so pay was decided by the teams, depending on what they could afford. Usually, there was more profit than loss, so the team enjoyed bonuses at the end of the financial year.

The final element, "the environment in which the self-organizing system operates," is a critical one which does require executive direction and involvement. It includes the standard computer systems needed to get work done, communication and conversation platforms, and any infrastructure necessary for all teams to operate effectively. They listen to where the organization wants to go and help it to get there. They disseminate ideas that teams come up with which might improve operations – but they do not command. They also look ahead and share their insights with the organization to see if they want to go there. Furthermore, executives need to represent the company to the outside world. Most importantly, they trust in self-organization and their people and stay out of the way.

The C-Suite mindset will be challenged by having to move from sequential and serial thinking to simultaneous and parallel thinking. Who makes a sale? Who markets? Who operates IT and makes IT decisions? Who procures? And ultimately, who decides what's best and what's next?

Furthermore, executives will be deeply challenged by self-managed teams and self-organizing systems. These question their authority, control, role, power, self-image, ego, and even their livelihood. It will take a strong and secure executive to undo their legacy and implement this very different way of running their organization.

NOTES

1 Andrew Spanyi, *Business Process Thinking*. www.1000ventures.com/business_ guide/process_thinking.html, [Accessed July 2019].
2 Dee W Hock, *As I See It*. www.deewhock.com/#intro, [Accessed July 2019].

3 Gareth Morgan, *Images of Organization* (updated ed.), SAGE, Thousand Oaks, CA, 2006.
4 Frederic Laloux, *Reinventing Organizations: A Guide to Creating Organizations Inspired by the Next Stage of Human Consciousness*, Nelson Parker, Mills, MA, 2014.
5 Terry White, *Reinventing the IT Department*, Routledge, Abingdon, UK, 2001.
6 Craig W Reynolds, Flocks, Herds, and Schools: A Distributed Behavioral Model (SIGGRAPH '87 Conference Proceedings), *Computer Graphics*, 21(4), 25–34, 1987.

CHAPTER NINE

What customers want yesterday

GENERATIONS OF CUSTOMERS

In the section on generational differences, we talked about different expectations, worldviews, and behaviors. These expectations and worldviews translate into customer requirements and market segments. As stated before, the division of generations and the association of behaviors with them is obviously a generalization, but viewing generations separately does help us understand how different cohorts of people think and act.

There is an older generation than baby boomers, and a younger generation than millennials (or Generation Y), but we haven't discussed them yet because we were looking only at those people who populated our organizations. The older generation is called the "Silent Generation," and the youngest generation is called the "Digital Teens," or "Generation Z," and each generation has different priorities, needs, and buying patterns. We'll summarize them in the next few paragraphs.

The Silent Generation was shaped by war and economic hardship. They value security and family and are mostly retired. While they spend most of their time at home, the vast majority use email and the internet to keep in contact with their families and friends. They will use a few applications that they know and like and will not change easily. They are impatient with floods of information and won't read unsolicited emails or sift through crowded websites. They are more "impulsive" and will buy something they think will suit them, rather than researching for further options.

Baby boomers grew up during a period of sustained economic growth and the start of the technological revolution. While they understand technology, they lived through its introduction to organizations and are somewhat suspicious of it and its promises. They know that technology improves operations but are cynical about its value and benefits. Baby boomers are the wealthiest generation and they like to spend their money. And given the aging population in the western world, they probably represent the most significant market at the moment. They don't want to fuss or spend time customizing a product, so they look for ready-made options and quick fixes. They like personalized service and are the most likely generation to abandon a purchase if they experience below par service. Only a small minority of baby boomers find shopping relaxing – they'll do their research, establish the price and quality they want, then go and get it. They know what they want and are unlikely to solicit references or check out reviews and ratings. They are unlikely to test new products, nor will they easily be diverted from the product they have decided they want. The vast majority shop in stores, and if a product is not in stock, they'll go somewhere else, rather than order online.

Generation X experienced the social and economic upheavals of the 1980s and beyond and are more cynical and skeptical about business. Being children of families with both parents working, they became self-reliant and believed that if something needs to be done, they would have to do it themselves. They are confident, pragmatic, resourceful, and adaptable. They are tech-savvy, conducting their research at home and shopping in person. Being independent and cynical, they want to be communicated with honestly, using clear product and marketing messages, with a simple and obvious path to purchase. They are price- and value-sensitive and want all price options made open to them – they hate price and service surprises and will drop a vendor if they feel they have been hoodwinked. They distrust large conglomerates (which is ironic as Gen X'ers started many of the tech corporations which dominate the world today) and are deeply cynical about advertisements. (This differs from millennials who just don't believe adverts at all.) Because of their autonomy, they like to feel in control of their purchasing decisions and want to be kept in the loop, both before and after their purchases. Most of their communications during the day are associated with work, and they do their research into products and services at night and their shopping during the day.

Millennials or Generation Y consumers are sometimes called "digital natives," having been brought up in an era of mature technologies at home and of new technologies being introduced at a more rapid rate. They are the largest generation in the workforce and have the spending power to support this. They are both digitally savvy and comfortable with tech. They have a multi-platform mindset and expect those who deal with them to have a presence and deal with them seamlessly, no matter what platform they work on. Millennials favor truth and authenticity and will view any idealized advertising with disfavor. In fact, they consider all adverts with distrust and view them as an invitation to research all products in the market at best. They research products intensely, placing a premium on ratings, reviews, and references from their online friends. Eight out of ten millennials won't buy anything without reading a review first. It is millennials who have resulted in the "influencer" phenomenon. These are people of social stature (often merely the number of online followers they have), who recommend a product, with the implication that if they use it, so should others. Marketers try to find influencers and pay them for supporting their products – there is even a micro-influencer move, using influencers with between 5 and 10,000 followers to target niche groups. Millennials prefer real-life, person-to-person approaches and representation of the products they consume. But beware, if they catch you out in falsehood, you're doomed – they will cut off all dealings with you, and even more importantly, will tell all their friends, contacts, and followers. Don't lie to millennials. They are highly educated and culturally diverse, more so than any other generation. But they are the first generation to have educational debt well into their thirties and can often not afford to move from the parental home. Therefore, they are price-sensitive (two-thirds will switch suppliers if they find a service that offers a more than 30% saving) and are often not in the market for homeware. Because millennials do not take suppliers too seriously, they respond to companies which use humor and who appear not to take themselves seriously either. They like videos that do not appear to advertise anything – a fact that fits well with millennials not approving of adverts in general. Having been raised in a connected world, they are impatient and expect instant service.

The newest generation (born after 2000), is now 19 years old and the "Generation Z" or "Digital Teens" is between 13 and 20 years old. They are always connected to the world around them – so much so that it's becoming dysfunctional in society. Their buying power is higher than we would expect, being about half the buying power of millennials (or much more according to some estimates), but they influence about eight times more spending in the family – 70% of the food buying decisions and 80-90% of items bought for them.

Marketing and selling to different generations obviously depend on the product you have to sell and the generations which you have targeted as customers. But "customers" come in different flavors – let's look at that.

TYPES OF CUSTOMERS

You have customers even before they buy from you. These are the potential customers who are in the market for your (or someone else's) product or service. In organizations where there is a sales team they are called leads and prospects: leads being someone who may be interested in what you have to sell and whom you have to approach, and prospects being people who have expressed an interest in your products or services. There is a third form of potential customer who you know nothing about but who is in "research mode" and looking to see who's out there to solve their problem. Let's call them unfamiliar customers, because they don't know about you and you don't know about them.

Unfamiliar customers need information above all else. Irrespective of their generation, they need information in depth. It's up to them how deep they want to go. One thing they don't need is bunkum and advertising gumpth. Honesty is appreciated by all generations, transparency even more. Several organizations generate trust by exposing their product, warts and all. Their message is: "If you were looking for instant solutions, then we're not for you. But if you want well-advised and guaranteed success, then we have the answer that you need." For most prospective customers this approach resonates well – "You can't have this, but you can have that."

Think about unfamiliar customers for a moment. You don't know them, but they are looking for information and they are also looking for guidance and help, both of which you can provide by satisfying their pre-buying needs: something for nothing. And you can allow for all of the above using a digital solution, especially the "something for nothing" requirement. While information is something for nothing obviously, a digital approach also allows you to provide guidance and help. Hints and tips, methods and recipes, comparisons, and ratings (especially honest ratings of competitive products) will all help customers feel that you are the place to go if they have a problem. Say a woodworker finds a website selling glues and fasteners, but that site also offers woodworking shortcuts and tips, provides templates for projects, and points them in the direction of products that they don't supply. The products from this website would probably be the first on their list, because prospective customers also want to see depth and breadth – that you're focused on their problem as a whole, rather than merely trying to sell them your glue/nails/screws. You're trying to help them with their problem, of which your product may be a small part. An unfamiliar customer becomes familiar with you and your product and then moves to be a potential customer or a "lead."

A potential customer still hasn't bought anything from you yet and needs to be handled in a specific way. While the need for information, guidance, and help is shared across all types of customers, the flavor changes from type to type. Prospective customers probably know a bit about your product, but now they're looking for options, and new perspectives ("Oh, I hadn't thought of it like that."). Above all, they do not want disagreeable surprises in the form of terms and conditions that disadvantage them, or incomplete solutions, or add-ons that are not included in the price. Prospective customers are trying to build confidence in you and your product, and most often are actually on your side … But, surprise them unpleasantly and you lose them. They want to be heard and understood, which means that they expect you to provide options and to help them avoid pitfalls and unsuitable solutions. Two other things that prospective customers are looking for is consistency and no repeats. This is critical to millennials and Generation Z (Gen Z) – they can find absolutely no excuse for having to tell their story twice, or for someone contradicting what another in your organization has said. Digital CRM (Customer Relationship Management) solutions should help with consistency and no repeats, among a bunch of other things, but up to 70% of CRM initiatives fail. Mostly because of patchy implementation – in terms of business processes, and in terms of user adoption. This is not a critique of CRM, but if it is patchily implemented, you'll find one part of the business not knowing about interactions that another part has had with a customer, and they'll be asking the customer to repeat themselves. If CRM is patchily adopted, you'll find some of your people not capturing what they've said to customers, so others may say something different and you'll be inconsistent. And no repeats and consistency are critical to all customer relationships. For millennials and Gen Z, and whether you have CRM or not, there is an expectation from anyone you deal with that you are up-to-date and ordered in the information that is available to them. Ultimately, potential customers want to feel confident in their choice of your product or service and to trust that you will deliver what you promise.

A new customer expects a smooth take-on experience – no surprises, repeats, transparency, and, above all, he or she does not want to experience buyer's remorse: Have they made the right decision to buy at all? Have they chosen the right product? What will others think? Can they afford the ongoing costs? … and on and on. This is where the service provider can have a positive impact – by assuring new customers of the wisdom of their decision, by offering added value immediately, by soliciting their input for both the purchase and for how they find working with you. It's a little like a first date with everyone feeling their way around what works and what doesn't. Here's the thing: 25% of people will drop the supplier after one bad experience, and 92% will drop out after three bad experiences (even loyal and long-standing customers). The ability to switch suppliers, to research and compare alternatives, and to match services and products is easy and becoming more so as time goes on. There are very few "locked-in" customers. After someone becomes a customer, it is all about the relationship. The three themes common to prospective, new, and loyal customers hold true: Transparency (no surprises), consistency (no repeats of contradictions), and personalization (customers are not a number, are listened to, and are understood). Customers are looking for empathy, which is different from sympathy, although both are important. Empathy is the ability to put yourself in someone else's shoes and doing so for a customer may mean that your staff may have to work outside company policy and procedure to collaborate to solve the customer's problem.

All of the above suggests that there is no single approach to customers. Across generations, but also within groups of similar customers, each has unique needs and relationship expectations. This further suggests that hard and fast rules will constrain rather than empower staff in their dealings with customers, which then reintroduces the concepts of self-managed teams and self-organizing systems, as discussed in Chapter 8. Offering staff guidelines and helping them achieve goals has to be more effective than a command-and-control management system. I think one of the contributors to the origination of command-and-control (other than the military (and church)) is that it just wasn't possible to manage in any other way back then. Apart from being the dominant culture at the time, there wasn't the technology to allow things to be done differently on a large scale. But also at the time, there wasn't the technology available to enable customers to research, compare, and buy other than by visiting stores and chatting to friends. Now the tech is available and is being used to permit customers to investigate every option, to have a worldwide view, to compare options and prices, to engage with suppliers no matter where they are, and to get opinions from experts and friends. And to do all of this in moments: Millennials tend to do all of this while standing in the store, before making a decision to buy. If the way of purchasing and making decisions to buy has changed so dramatically, then surely the method of selling and helping customers decide to buy must change dramatically as well.

IF CUSTOMERS BUY DIFFERENTLY, THEN SUPPLIERS SHOULD SELL DIFFERENTLY

This could turn into a lesson on customer relationships or customer experience (CX), but that's not the purpose. Instead, I merely want to show some of the (many) areas of business that should change to meet customer buying behaviors. Digitalization helps in all of them because customers have adopted digitalization in all fields in which they buy – the younger customers more than the older ones. So let's give a few examples.

Suppliers should be everywhere – on all channels. Sounds easy, but first, remember that most decision-makers in organizations are Generation X who grew up with Facebook and Twitter and probably think that a presence on these is sufficient. And while 85% of millennials and Gen Zs use social networking for their purchase decision making, they often use different social networking platforms. Snapchat is used by Gen Z far more than Facebook. Millennials still use Facebook but, increasingly, also use Instagram. Generation X and baby boomers like Facebook but also use Pinterest. All of this ignores Tumblr, Whatsapp, QZone, QQ, and many other social networking apps that are on the rise. So, when decisions about what channels to use to connect to customers are made, perhaps these should be made by younger decision-makers, backed up by research. Who makes decisions in your organization should depend on the type and age of the customers about which the decision is to be made.

Suppliers should answer quickly. Most customers expect that if they post a question, comment, review or complaint on any one of a supplier's channels, then there should be an answer within 60 minutes. And this expectation is a 24/7 expectation. Office hours just don't exist in modern online customers' minds. (Facebook considers a business to be "quick" or "very responsive" if they answer within 5 minutes around the clock). This suggests having a constant monitoring service, but mostly this can be done digitally. However, the response must be made by a person, although Robotic Process Automation is starting to take up the slack here. There are some decisions to be made as well – do you respond in public or in private? Usually, a public comment would be answered publicly, even if it's merely an acknowledgment with a promise to get back to the customer in private. Some experts recommend only replying in public twice – there's a danger of the conversation turning into a flame war. So answer publicly twice, the second answer inviting the specific customer to move to a private channel. The speed of solutions can be significantly increased by digital methods, but ultimately, you need a person who has the freedom to decide how to answer and what kind of response you should make. There's no doubt though that you can't run a command and control decision-making model here.

Suppliers should provide self-service as far as possible, and that's pretty far. One example is in the servicing of a motorcar – there are a few apps available where the details and service history of a car is captured, and which schedules services for the customer, based on their approval of the proposed service date. Once the customer agrees, the vehicle is automatically booked in and the customer brings the car, leaves the keys, and that's it. No phone calls, filling out forms, and so on. Another example is the self-service chatbot, which allows customers to explore options through a "wizard" (a natural-language AI-controlled conversational tool), which guides the customer towards making a decision. The chatbot must also allow for the customer to move to a person at the touch of a button. The most obvious example of self-service is FAQs (frequently asked questions) but be aware that merely posting 15 FAQs and forgetting them is very dangerous – if a customer doesn't find an answer, they should be able to get hold of a live agent fast. Also, FAQs should be continuously updated. Live agents should record which questions get asked often and posted to the FAQ portal. The FAQs should be monitored and scheduled to appear in order of the frequency with which they are asked. Again, this is not a tutorial on self-service, but it does highlight that although 73% of customers prefer to help themselves, the path to clunky or poor service is a short one, unless you apply some deep thinking and sophistication.

Selling to digitally astute customers is more than putting your product catalog online. You need to think through the customer journey – all the touchpoints that a customer has with your organization from before you even know about them, through their entire journey when dealing with your company. Traditionally, the customer journey followed Michael Porter's value chain: Marketing made your product known to unfamiliar customers; Sales addressed leads and converted them into customers;

Order fulfillment made sure the customer got what they had bought; and so it goes on. But not today. As I said in the previous chapter, the simple task of purchasing shoes online involved a customer dealing with up to six departments at the same time, through a total of 31 touchpoints. It's not sequential, or even logical, and if you are to sell to digitally savvy customers, most of your business processes, indeed your culture, need to change.

CHAPTER TEN

Business ecosystems change everything

BUSINESS ECOSYSTEMS

James Moore coined the term "business ecosystem" in 1993, in a
Harvard Business Review article: "Predators and Prey: A New Ecology of
Competition."[1] He describes a business ecosystem as a collection of related
companies, sometimes in the same industry, which co-evolve capabilities
around a new innovation. These companies operate both as competition
and in cooperation to satisfy customer needs and support new products.
Moore said that although networks were a conventional business concept,
they did not help managers understand the complex systemic forces at play
in business environments. He further states that our thinking is limited by
linear, competitive, and static thinking – radical ideas indeed, considering
that 36 years later we still run organizations as linear, competitive, and
static structures: We define linear processes and believe in management
by control and that a pyramidical structure is the way that we will succeed
(See Chapter 8 for much more detail).

But back to Moore's ecosystem idea: By describing business as an
ecosystem, he introduces the notion of self-organization, of relatedness
both as competition or in cooperation, and of natural selection. He talks
of co-evolution, complexity, and proposed that it is competition between
ecosystems, not individual companies, that transforms business. There has
been some criticism of Moore's business ecosystem idea, primarily that
Moore says that there must be a leader – where most ecologists suggest
that there is no individual "organ of control"[2] in an ecosystem and that an
ecosystem can be deliberately constructed by the leader. I agree with this
critique – ecosystems don't have self-appointed leaders, but several lessons
can be taken from thinking about businesses as part of an ecosystem.

Your organization is part of a business ecosystem, whether you recognize it
or not. Your customers and suppliers are part of your ecosystem, obviously,
as are your competitors. And your suppliers are not only those people or
companies with which you have an agreement to provide the materials
needed to build and deliver your product. Supplies also include electricity,
computers, office stationery, and any service you have outsourced as being

non-core. Your ecosystem includes your bank and shareholders, and the makers of complementary products that are used in conjunction with your own (food with drink, batteries with torches, hardware with software, a product with packaging). Regulatory agencies and the media are also part of your ecosystem. At this stage, it might be tempting to throw up your hands and proclaim that *everything* is part of your ecosystem, so what is the point? And there you would be making the error that many organizations have made and which results in less efficiency and more competition today than is necessary, because ecosystems are firstly interrelated – every element mentioned above is related to how you conduct business. Every part has an effect on how you do business. And anything which affects a component of your ecosystem can affect your company.

An example of ecosystems are banking systems, mainly if supported by an application that also allows for paying bills, hotel and travel bookings, access to promotions, and, of course, managing accounts. Other examples include Amazon, which has disrupted retail through their partnerships, taxi applications which link taxi owners and drivers to customers, or HealthHiway, an Indian online health network which connects over 1,000 hospitals, 10,000 doctors, and more than 1,100 hospitals, pharmacies, medical insurance, and laboratories to provide a healthcare ecosystem.

ECOSYSTEM THINKING

Ecosystem thinking can help you understand and plan for your business strategy. The ecosystem is almost always represented as a network or a web of relationships. There is a hierarchy in an ecosystem, sometimes of predatory and prey, and sometimes of dependencies or, perhaps, partnerships. (Even the predator/prey relationship is a dependency, because if the prey dies out, so do the predators.) An ecosystem takes place in an environment, has "actors" (components), and flows (usually energy). The ecosystem co-evolves to try to create a state of equilibrium. In a business ecosystem, the hierarchy is defined by the roles that the individual business actors play and the influence or power that they have to effect change on other actors. This power limits the choices that are available to the actors: They can make deliberate choices, trying to change other business actors actively; they make emergent choices, reacting to emerging conditions; or, they can have constrained choices based on what "rules" the more powerful actors impose. Remember that government or industry bodies are actors in most ecosystems.

Marko Karhiniemi[3] proposes five steps in analyzing a business ecosystem:

1. Analyze the environment in which the ecosystem operates, including the political, social, economic, and technological background.
2. Analyze how the business ecosystem works, looking at the various layers – usually the digital network, the applications, systems and API's (Application Programming Interfaces), the standards and policies that govern behavior, and the business domains. Each of these can be represented as a layer within the ecosystem. Also, look at the measures of health and the success of the ecosystem.
3. Analyze entities and the roles of existing primary players in the ecosystem, including your own organization. These roles can be defined as:

    3.1. Niche roles – these are the bulk of the ecosystem and specialize in their own area of expertise.
    3.2. Keystone roles – those players whose success or failure will cascade to other areas of the ecosystem.
    3.3. Dominators – these players control or try to control as much of the ecosystem as they can. They buy those niche players who create value that they want to create for themselves, or who take profits that they want for themselves.
    3.4. Hub landlords – these businesses do not add value. Instead, they extract it where they can. Holding companies fit this category.
    3.5. Look at the transactions and exchanges (tangible and intangible) within the ecosystem between the entities such as:

        3.5.1. Payments
        3.5.2. Documents like invoices, schedules, and orders

3.5.3. Equipment and products

3.5.4. Advice and feedback

3.6. Analyze how the ecosystem is changing. Look at changing:

3.6.1. Roles – for instance, are keystones trying to become dominators, etc?

3.6.2. Technologies – is there a new technology that will make cooperation easier?

3.6.3. Business modes – who creates value, who adds to it, who takes profit?

While this is relatively straightforward, some concepts need to be explained (not too much though – read Karhiniemi's paper for more detail).

There are some critical lessons to learn here, which can affect how you operate in the ecosystem. Firstly, the actions of one player affect the other players depending on their role. Secondly, your success depends on the ecosystem's success. Thirdly, it's not about the industry but about the ecosystem in which you operate. Fourthly, in ecosystems, it's about the flow of value, and finally, your understanding of the ecosystem's dynamics will affect your commercial and strategic success.

An example of a business ecosystem may make this analysis process clearer. A cell-phone manufacturer needs software to run on the phone, carriers (mobile telecommunications companies), the internet, applications developers, content providers, cell-phone and online stores, and the end-users themselves. In this instance, the mobile manufacturer is probably a niche player, while the carrier is a keystone player. Applications developers are niche players, and the internet is a keystone to the success of the product. There are regulations that the manufacturer must conform to, and the end-user is part of a social and economic environment. Other cell-phone manufacturers may be forcing technological change in the background. Understanding these elements and the forces at play can inform or even drive the cell-phone manufacturer's strategy. They should be asking the question of how they maintain and protect their niche. What formal partnerships should they craft with keystone or dominant players? And how do we capture value – make sure that a significant portion of the value that we create stays in the business?

HOW ECOSYSTEMS CHANGE EVERYTHING

Analysts talk of two types of value in an ecosystem: Value creation and value capture. Value creation is when a business makes something or adds to the value of something already made. Packaging and distribution add to the value of a product that has already been made. (Remember that packaging can be digital as well as physical – for example, a website that shows customers the features of a product and how to use it, is packaging that adds to the product's value.) Value capture is a crucial issue for you. Basically, value captured is the gross profit that you make – you may create value, but if you are required by your ecosystem to sell your product at a minimal profit, or if your processes are inefficient, the value that you capture may be insufficient to upgrade your production processes, and you may be facing insolvency. One can capture value without creating it – a good example is tax and rent. Or you can capture value far over the cost of creating it – a best-selling book is a good example, where the author puts in a fixed amount of work and benefits for years.

During the industrial revolution producing companies were trying to maximize economies of scale. The larger and more standardized they could become, the lower the unit price for them. Of course, they could capture value by keeping their prices as high as the market would bear. The emphasis was on the supply side of the equation, to capture value. In the digital, networked, ecosystem age, the power shifts to the demand side, and value is captured not because of how big and efficient you are (although efficiency certainly adds to captured value), but instead you capture value by how extensive your network and ecosystem is, and how quickly you can respond to demand requirements. This is why many organizations have become "customer-centric," to sense demand changes and respond as promptly as possible. Value is created in the network (for instance, if you have 10,000 customers, and you sell these contacts to complementary products, which is captured value, you are creating nothing new, yet drawing revenue from your network).

In a digital economy, networks and ecosystems are not only more accessible, but they are also the drivers of business. And while efficiency and scale are useful inside your organization, it is the efficiency of the ecosystem and the extent of the network that defines your success. Captured value leverages "network effects," where a product or service gains more value as more people use it. A good example is a cell-phone network or a social networking application. The higher the number of people using a product or service, the greater the lock-in of those users. This is when it becomes prohibitively costly to the user to change to another product or service. A classic example is the QWERTY keyboard. This keyboard layout originated with the old manual typewriters. In the early days, as people became faster at typing, the manufacturers found that the key arms became jammed if pressed at the same time or in quick succession. The typewriter manufacturer reconfigured the keyboard so that commonly used letters were spaced as far from each other as possible, to slow down typing speeds. There are much more efficient keyboard layouts like the Dvorak keyboard, which was designed to increase typing speed and the Colemak keyboard, which is designed to provide a bridge between the QWERTY layout and the Dvorak one. But because of lock-in, very few people use either of the more efficient versions. The costs of changing designs and, more significantly, of every person who types having to learn a new layout, prevent the more efficient products being adopted. An ecosystem tries to create lock-in – think about the Apple/Microsoft lock-in. Microsoft is winning, as Apple has to develop import and export programs to allow users to use or transfer documents to Microsoft users. Notice that Microsoft has not developed Apple compatibility.

Here's the bottom line in thinking about ecosystems as against industry groupings. Understanding and leveraging your ecosystem is more important than going it alone. The emphasis has switched from suppliers to customers, and only ecosystems can keep pace at an economically viable rate.

NOTES

1 James F Moore, *Predators and Prey: A New Ecology of Competition*, Harvard Business Review, May-June 1993.
2 G Koenig, Le Concept D'écosystème D'affaires Revisité, *M@n@gement*, 15(2), 209–224, 2012.
3 Marko Karhiniemi, *Creating and Sustaining Successful Business Ecosystems*, Helsinki School of Economics, Helsinki, 2009. https://core.ac.uk/download/pdf/80700187.pdf, [Accessed August 2019].

PART 2

The evolving C-Suite

The first part of this book examined the challenges facing C-Suite executives. This second part offers suggestions on how the C-Suite should respond to these and other challenges. There is no single answer, and the power is in the hands of the C-Suite. So this part can only be suggestions. And also there are several approaches that one can take. The first step, however, is to be convinced that it is necessary, even critical, to change the way the organization and the C-Suite works. Then one can go the "big-bang" route, or one can evolve. Evolving is a "sense and respond" strategy, and allows for incremental change, which, given the other changes happening in the environment, is probably the way to go.

The structure of Part 2 is slightly different from Part 1. The C-Suite ability to meet the challenges depends on how they think. That is superimposed on everything. If the mindset of C-Suite executives is a resistant one, or if they believe in a window-dressing approach, the organization and the C-Suite will not evolve. Well, it will, but towards what I believe to be a dystopian future for themselves and their organization. What the C-Suite does and its skills and attributes are interlinked. And while the organization and the C-Suite will evolve at the same time, the chapter on "The evolved organization" sets the stage for the evolution of the C-Suite.

CHAPTER ELEVEN

The mind and motivations of the C-Suite

HISTORY OF THE C-SUITE

Jacques Neatby[1] tells us that in the 1950s, Alfred Sloan of General Motors brought together the heads of several business units to address company-wide issues. In the 1970s, this began to change to something more like the executive teams we see today, with the idea being to centralize decision-making, coordinate across business activities, and to provide decision-making support to the CEO.

Neatby reports that executive teams were growing to an average size of ten members, double their size of 30 years ago. Two commonly cited reasons for this growth are to retain executives and to bring additional perspectives to the decision-making team. There are several downsides, not the least being wasting time as often more than 50% of discussions do not affect many team members. Also, the CEO has to act as a referee because of the many perspectives now available, and if we add in ego and personal priorities, then a referee is a must. The growth of the C-Suite has primarily been with functional managers instead of general managers,[2] so the departmental priority problem is compounded (as Neatby says, the CEO has become a Chief Mediation Officer). An allied issue is that staff see infighting in the expanded C-Suite and collaboration across departments drops. And all of this makes decisions take longer, a situation that threatens organizations in a digital world.

WHAT IS THE C-SUITE?

The C-Suite is made up of "C" level executives, where mostly their titles involve the word "Chief," as in Chief Executive Officer (CEO), Chief Financial Officer, Chief Operating Officer, and so on. Airbnb has a Chief Trust Officer, and titles in other organizations include the Chief Ecosystems Officer, Chief Happiness Officer, and Chief Freelance Relations Officer. It seems there is no shortage of chiefs. In Britain, the Managing Director is synonymous with the CEO, and in America,

Presidents and Vice Presidents rule, OK? A chief is the head of an organized body of people – the person with the highest authority. Unfortunately, some C-Suite executives also think the adjective describes them as the most critical, authoritative or significant. This can have some ego implications as we will discuss later.

No matter what, having a C-Suite reinforces the hierarchy, and as we discussed in Chapter 1, Simon Caulkin said: "…managers are still building mass-production organizations fit for the early twentieth century, based on hierarchy, standardization, and compliance, rather than flexible, human-centered outfits…" We also discussed the fact that hierarchies reinforce power structures, and that standardization and compliance are probably not what business needs anymore. In the previous chapter, we saw that production organizations striving for economies of scale are changing to niche producers striving for network effects and that the emphasis has shifted from supply-side economics and requirements to demand-side economics and customer demands. I wonder if we need a C-Suite in modern businesses, and we'll get to that in the following chapters. For now, let's have a look at a generalized C-Suite.

With 70% of the C-Suite and 95% of CEOs being male, we are not being sexist when we refer to executives as "he." And with the average age of executives moving from 42 in 2012 to 48 in 2016, and the age of CEOs moving from 55 to 60 in the same period,[3] we can hardly call them young, or getting younger. Finally, when 72% of executives from the Fortune 500 companies are white, we have a profile of the C-Suite. Yes, I know these are generalizations but think for a moment what kind of thinking and decisions are being made by executives in a digital world. When over half of the workforce are millennials (digital natives), and most of middle-management are Generation X (who were the first kids to grow up with computers in their homes), there must be a disconnect between the decision-makers (conservative, command and control, hierarchy dependent), the executors of decisions (independent, cynical, distrust authority), and the workforce (digital natives, anti-hierarchy). In a digital world where flexibility and rapid response is a factor of survival,

WOMs (white, old, males – my term) might not be the best leadership that organizations need. At the start of this book, I said: "Let's talk about revolution, then let's talk about power." So let's talk. There is a revolution in business, driven primarily by digital technology and changing attitudes, but the power resides with the WOMs. So perhaps we should look at how WOMS think, as executives and decision-makers. I'll refer to executives in the C-Suite as males (because most of them are), but females are also included, where applicable.

THE PSYCHOLOGY OF THE C-SUITE

When you do the research on the psychology of executives, you come up with titles like "The dark side of executive psychology," "Executive derailment," and "1 in 5 CEOs are psychopaths." Wow! All of these are based on academic research. There are positive papers, but almost all of them advise that there is a need for executive psychology to be examined and managed.

To be fair, "The dark side of executive psychology" is actually a paper called "Beyond the dark side of executive psychology,"[4] which examines the fascination that researchers have with executive hubris (arrogant pride inviting downfall). The researchers study how rigorous the assumptions about executive hubris are, and do not suggest that it doesn't exist, instead advising that terms should be defined better and that measurement of it should improve. Executive hubris (arrogant pride) is dangerous to businesses because CEOs want to take over other companies and embark on ambitious projects – which is not necessarily a bad thing, it's just that the thinking motivations behind this might be suspect. For the moment, and from personal experience, I'm going to assume that executive hubris is real and is a threat to organizations. Interestingly, when researchers look at executive hubris, they also look at narcissism, which is defined as excessive self-love and vanity and generally associated with an infantile level of personality development.

Narcissism, especially in CEOs, may be a defensive trait. If you grade CEO performance, the average performance would be 22 out of 100.[5] So there's a 78% chance that people will think that the CEO isn't performing well. (See Chapter 12 on why CEOs shouldn't be doing the job they think they should be doing, to understand why people grade their performance so poorly.) But, in the face of constant criticism, CEOs might become narcissistic (No-one loves me so I'll love myself). And a touch of arrogant pride might support this narcissism.

Caution is, surprisingly, also a negative trait for executives. Appropriate caution is fine, but too many executives, when faced with a decision are also faced with several factors that mitigate against taking that decision. Firstly, it's always complex, and the information available is never sufficient. My old CEO used to say that if you had all the information, then there's no decision to be made. Decisions involve doubt and choices. Secondly, the risks and stakes are always high – or else the decision would have been taken by someone else. Thirdly, time is an issue – often because the decision has taken a while to get to the executive team, or things have been left unaddressed until they become a critical problem. The time that executives have to consider the decision is also a factor – most execs are too busy to think (which is another problem for the C-Suite – they try to do too much). As a result of complexity, risks, and time, many executives do nothing or rely on past ideals and mentalities.

Another negative trait (we'll focus on positive attributes in a moment), is a focus on the wrong thing. Many executives and CEOs focus on profits, shareholders, and the executive team's priorities. In a digital world, a focus on customer needs, rapid change, and a driving vision that staff will buy into are more crucial to the success of the business. A focus on profits leads to cost-cutting or reducing customer services. When decisions need to be made about capital expenditure or new projects, ROI (return on investment) and risk are primary concerns of most C-Suites. While these are definitely factors that must be considered, successful executives make their decisions based on whether the expenditure or initiative fits the vision and strategy, while meeting customer needs. If they do that, the risks become manageable, and the profits will flow. A focus on shareholders is useful but not critical. Charles Handy defined six stakeholders in a business: Shareholders, staff, customers, suppliers, the community, and the environment. A single focus is dangerous, and the order of focus is the issue. I would suggest that the order should be customers, staff, suppliers, community, environment, and shareholders. In the first section of this chapter, I dealt with the fact that executive teams have doubled in size in the last 30 years and have become staffed with functional experts. This leads to multiple perspectives on what is needed for successful operations and, consequently, in-fighting and politics prevail. I know of an executive who, when she was promoted to a toxic and highly political exec team, hired a private detective to get the dirt on her team members so that she could get her way. This is extreme, but she needed to get work done and sought to achieve her goals in this political environment. (We had to meet at coffee shops because her office was bugged.) All of this was highly unsavory, of course, but it reinforces the point that executives may spend too much time contending with other executives to do their jobs properly.

One final negative trait worth considering is the belief that executives and CEOs can control everything. Perhaps before digitalization and the change of concentration from supply to demand requirements this was possible. But customers demand attention and the meeting of their needs, and to make this possible, decisions need to be devolved to the customer-facing elements of the business. Business is too complicated and moves too rapidly for the executive team to set themselves up as the controlling factor in the organization. Instead, they should concentrate on leadership and guidance so that decisions can be taken at the right level, for the right reasons. In Chapter 8, I discussed self-organizing systems and self-managed teams, where very few decisions are made by the executive team, and in some cases, almost no decisions are made at all. This is possible, and even desirable, given the complexity and pace of business.

The positive traits required by executives include vision, communication, integrative thinking, leadership, the ability to contend with complexity, and the ability to motivate others to work towards a goal. They also need courage, humility, and self-awareness.

In Chapter 4, I briefly touched on Warren Bennis's distinction between leadership and management, so let's start there because it encapsulates most of the positive traits that successful executives have. Bennis talks about leadership being "MAST," and management being "POEM." MAST stands for meaning, attention, self, and trust, while POEM stands for plan, organize, execute, and monitor. Executives need to have both in traditional organizations, but in self-managed organizations, they only need MAST. "Meaning" includes vision and integrative thinking, as well as contending with complexity. "Attention" includes communication and the ability to get others to work towards a goal. Finally, "self" and "trust" are leadership traits that include courage, humility, and self-awareness.

"Vision" is an overused concept in management theory, which is why I prefer "Meaning." I covered this in Chapter 4, but in summary: Executives need to make sense of the world and the demands placed on the organization by stakeholders (remember there are at least six of them). This perception of the world and stakeholders must then be filtered for what it means to their organization. For instance, in Australia, the government realized that their citizens were more astute with digital technologies than they were and that citizens expected to deal with government through digital channels. They embarked on a digitization and digitalization program to address this gap and serve their citizens better. (Remember that digitization is about converting records and documents to digital form, and digitalization involves creating the apps and training the people to work in a digital environment – I covered this in Chapter 5.) So the Australian government's vision was directed by the perception that they lagged their citizens digitally, and it meant that they needed to catch up and surpass their citizens in the digital space. So vision is the interpretation of the world and customer requirements, understanding what that means for the organization, and crafting a message that others will buy into.

Communication and getting others to work towards a goal is about grabbing the attention of the organization – both the decision-makers and the staff in general. Communication is not merely being able to talk or write in a message that others will understand. There's a step required before you open your mouth or put pen to paper. It is about conceptualizing the issue and creating a mental model that others will buy into – it's a worldview, but, importantly, it is also is concerned with whether others will see things in that way and act on what they see. I'll deal with executive communication in Chapter 13. By the way, true leaders don't believe that getting others to work towards a goal ever comes to giving commands. They are aware that Generation X distrusts authority and are cynical, and millennials need to be motivated to work in a particular way – giving orders is not going to cut it. Warren Bennis's MAST model of leadership includes "self," and "trust." These are closely linked – if an executive manages himself in a way that others appreciate, then their trust in him is improved.

One paper mentioned at the beginning of this section is called: "Beyond the dark side of executive psychology,"[6] where the authors look at executive hubris. They do suggest that the step beyond researching hubris is the executive "self," which may provide more positive leads in executive self-development. They define four elements of the executive self, which, when taken as a whole, presents a positive platform for executives to develop. The four components are personality (who they are and how they behave), self-concept (what they know about themselves and how they think), identity (their social/professional identity and how they relate to others), and body (how they feel and how they manage their health). That just about covers it. If an executive behaves in a combative way, their staff and others may act in the same way – silos in organizations are, in my opinion, initiated and sustained by executive behavior. Bollaert and Petit, in the above paper, talk about the "false self" and the "true self," which leads them to the concept of executive authenticity. If an executive is authentic, then they exhibit their true self and this, in turn, increases trust in them. However, the researchers also note that many executives exhibit an aversion to introspection, and being coached or analyzed, for fear that their false self will emerge. A dictionary definition of "trust" is the reliance on the integrity, strength, and ability of a person. It causes confidence in that person.

THE CHALLENGES OF BEING AN EXECUTIVE

Michael Porter, Jay Lorsch, and Nitin Nohria wrote an article[7] for *Harvard Business Review*, in which they show that seven surprises are waiting for new CEOs. The first surprise is that a CEO can't run the company. The pressures on his time are too great to take a hand in operational matters, and external demands like analysts, shareholders, and the media, keep him busy almost all the time anyway. The CEO must delegate if he is to survive. The second surprise is that they shouldn't give orders, except in rare cases. If the CEO has delegated appropriately, he should only have to approve decisions and not make them himself or advise that there may be another solution that should be investigated. Also, wielding direct power contradicts the first surprise. Finally, many CEOs find that if they make a decision, their calendar fills up with others wanting decisions, often bypassing his delegated person. On rare occasions, if a decision needs to be made, the CEO should do so in participation with the executive team. Participation means presenting your reasoning, listening to others, changing if appropriate, and securing the support of the executive team. I won't go through all seven surprises that Porter et al. presented, except for one, which was: "You are always sending a message." This applies to all executives in the C-Suite. Just the promotion to the C-Suite is a message. If an engineer takes over an engineering company, that's fine, but if a lawyer is promoted to the position, there will be rumors that the company is facing litigation. The car you drive, the clothes you wear, and its location and the size of your office all send messages. I once mishandled setting up a self-managed team in my company, because the message was that I couldn't manage them myself and wasn't prepared to take the hard decisions. CEOs can't afford to have speculative conversations with employees because they might send out a message of being indecisive, or someone might latch onto an idea and treat it as policy. We come back to the management of self – how executives behave and relate to others are all messages.

One of the significant challenges facing executives is the workload. Many execs work 50 to 60 hours a week. Again, this is because they are not delegating and trusting others. Also, they misunderstand their role as an executive. As a leader in the organization, they should be doing very little managing and more leading. Overwork often leads to health and, sometimes, marriage problems. Knowing that one is working too hard is easy but having the self-awareness and courage to change the workload is challenging. Pride and narcissism also play a part in overwork.

Limiting beliefs are a challenge to executives. One, which is that "I can do everything necessary," has been covered above – the simple answer is that you can't plan, organize, execute, and monitor everything. Successful executives believe that they should do as little of this as possible to make space for their leadership role. A second limiting belief is that: "I can find a solution to everything." Change that to "We can find a solution" and we're getting somewhere. An executive should guide and advise others in finding solutions rather than try to do it all themselves. Another is: "The past is a good informant of future actions." If this book teaches anything, it is that in a digital world, the past is probably the worst indicator of what will be successful in the future. The issue with limiting beliefs is because of the way we constrain ourselves in some way. I'll deal with limiting beliefs in more detail Chapter 15.

HOW THE C-SUITE THINKS

In general (and again, we're dealing with generalities, not minorities), the thinking of old white males dominates the C-Suite. Most are baby boomers and older Generation X, which means that they were not part of the digital revolution. However, in this chapter, we've talked extensively about the traits and challenges of being a C-Suite executive. The positive traits of executives are (or should be):

- Vision: Motivate for a desirable future state.
- Leadership: Direct and guide people.

- Communication: Conceptualize an issue and make others aware and informed.
- Integrative thinking: Bring disparate ideas, factors, and people together.
- Motivation: Get others to work towards a goal.
- Courage: Take on difficult and personally threatening issues.
- Humility: Be modest, courteous, and have a lack of false pride.
- Self-awareness: Understand one's own personality, behavior, identity, and relations with others.

Research shows that many executives exhibit some negative traits as well:

- Hubris: Arrogant pride inviting failure, leading to grand but rash decisions.
- Narcissism: Vanity – believing in one's rightness and ability to do everything.
- Overly cautious: Unable to make decisions with complex factors and incomplete information.
- Incorrectly focused: Profit and shareholders secondary to customer needs and good leadership.
- Control: Belief that they can control and manage everything in the business.

One can see that several negative traits directly contradict the positive ones. While this is definitely not true of all executives, given the average profile, one would be forgiven in saying that old white males may be overly cautious, incorrectly focused, and want to control everything – given that this was perhaps how they were managed before they became executives themselves. Hubris and narcissism may be there as well.

Successful executives' thinking was studied by Daniel Isenberg,[8] and he found that they think about processes and a few main problems at any one time. Given that this research was conducted before 1984, before the internet and digital business, his findings may be incompatible with the current business environment, but we should look at these two thinking modes: Firstly, the processes executives think about are mainly human processes and not business processes – how to bring people and groups together to deal with problems and take action. They try to think about the strengths and weaknesses of people, what's important to them, and what their priorities are. Secondly, executives think about a few problems at a time. Interestingly, Isenberg found that executives think about problems that are easier to solve, rather than which issues are the most important to address. In dealing with these two thinking modes, executives use intuition more than one would expect, spend a lot of time understanding what the problem is, dealing with ambiguity, and contending with surprises.

Given the rapidly changing business environment, which includes globalization, connectivity and scrutiny, shifts in technology which will affect business, and new customer expectations, past experience is no longer a reliable guide for future action. So an executive needs innovative thinking, adaptability, and the ability to deal with paradoxes or contradictory truths. Included in this ability to think about the future without depending on past experience, is the need to renew themselves continually. If one includes Isenberg's findings that executives are concerned with human processes, then they must also reinvent how their organization works together to deal with the rapidly changing business environment. And when we are talking about organizational change, executives need to reconsider the command and control hierarchy of which they are part. They need to think about who holds power (the customer), who makes decisions (people closest to the customer), who initiates change and manages business processes (self-managed teams), and who identifies problems facing the organization (the staff). Again, executives need to adopt a leadership role rather than a management role in their organizations.

The challenges facing executives, where they need to provide leadership, are outlined in the chapters in the first part of this book. So they need to be thinking about how their staff is educated and how to mitigate problems inherent with current educational systems. They need to think about the different generations in their organization and how to motivate them using their own priorities. Executives need to make sense of the information flood and to be able to sense changes in the business environment, technology, and customer requirements. There needs to be some serious thinking done about how they will use digital products and services to improve the way their organization competes and meets customer needs. Technology has changed the economy, society, the environment, and, of course, business. Executives need to make sense of that and visualize a path for their organization to navigate these changes.

There's more than enough thinking and leadership required from executives to fill their working day – so we come to their role in the organization – it's about guiding their business, not about managing it.

NOTES

1 Jacques Neatby, The Ballooning Executive Team, *Harvard Business Review*, 2016. https://hbr.org/2016/07/the-ballooning-executive-team, [Accessed August 2019].

2 Maria Guadalupe, Li Hongyi, and Julie Wulf, Who Lives in the C-suite? Organizational Structure and the Division of Labor in Top Management, *Harvard Business School*, 2013. http://hbs.edu/faculty/Publication%20Files/12-059_040a5ca7-f80c-4d01-abd3-57f431795613.pdf, [Accessed August 2019].

3 Oliver Staley, How the Average Age of CEOs and CFOs Has Changed Since 2012, *Quartz*, 2017. https://qz.com/1074326/how-the-average-age-of-ceos-and-cfos-has-changed-since–2012/, [Accessed August 2019].

4 Helen Bollaert and Vale´rie Petit, Beyond the Dark Side of Executive Psychology: Current Research and New Directions, *European Management Journal*, 28, 2010.

5 Sarah Lacey, What's the Most Difficult CEO Skill? *Techcrunch*, 2011. https://techcrunch.com/2011/03/31/what%E2%80%99s-the-most-difficult-ceo-skill-managing-your-own-psychology/, [Accessed July 2019].

6 Helen Bollaert and Vale´rie Petit, Beyond the Dark Side of Executive Psychology: Current Research and New Directions, *European Management Journal*, 28, 2010.

7 Michael Porter, Jay Lorsch, and Nitin Nohria, Seven Surprises for New CEOs, *Harvard Business Review*, 2004. https://hbr.org/2004/10/seven-surprises-for-new-ceos, [Accessed July 2019].

8 Daniel Isenberg, How Senior Managers Think, *Harvard Business Review*, 1984. https://hbr.org/1984/11/how-senior-managers-think [Accessed June 2019].

CHAPTER TWELVE

The role of the C-Suite

In Chapter 15, I'll talk about how an evolved C-Suite approaches things. The ideas and methods are so different from current C-Suite practices that the team will need to evolve in that direction. They need a starting point, and this chapter provides some ideas about relatively small and safe changes. There are several steps that existing teams and individuals can and should take to accommodate the current business reality, and they will provide a platform from which to evolve.

PEOPLE, POWER, AND POLITICS

Looking at current descriptions of C-Suite executives, one comes across comments like: "They are the most powerful and influential people in any company"; "They occupy the corner offices"; and "They usually have the most experience and the highest responsibilities." Power, influence, and responsibility predominate. The corner office is usually given to executives because they have two windows, as opposed to one window or none at all. It's about status, although how a team works when they have offices at opposite corners of the building, I'm not sure. In Japan, C-Suite executives often sit at the center of the building so that they can communicate easily with each other and they are accessible to their staff. I've talked about conflict and divisive perspectives in the C-Suite and would imagine that putting them together instead of as far apart as physically possible might be a way of reducing friction. The implications of corner offices might suggest that these executives are chiefs of a physical domain and that their role is functional rather than concerned with the performance of the organization as a whole. Corner offices lend the lie to the C-Suite being a coherent team.

The C-Suite consists of executives who usually have a title beginning with "Chief …" The usual team is headed by a Chief Executive Officer (CEO) and, by modern standards, an average of ten other "C's." This is a large team to coordinate, and if they all located in the corners, this is undoubtedly made more difficult. In Chapter 11, I mentioned that Neatby considered the doubling in size of the C-Suite, and how research by Guadalupe et al. showed that this growth was mainly in functional executives (people representing their function in the organization). In this circumstance, the CEO might become the Chief Mediation Officer who tries to arbitrate between executives and the different perspectives that they bring to the team.

One of the "surprises" for executives that Michael Porter posited was: "You are always sending a message." What messages are being sent by corner offices, differing perspectives, and the need to mediate them, and executives representing their functional specialization rather than the whole company?

I think the C-Suite is an essential part of any organization, as a leadership, thinking, and guidance team. But also as a team that interacts with the external world – customers, shareholders, the media, suppliers, the community, and importantly, the environment in which the organization operates. And here we see the role of the C-Suite in the digital age. The world, technology, business, and society are changing faster than ever before. So, attitudes and roles which applied to "before" cannot have currency in the C-Suite. This doesn't mean experience is not useful, it is, but it should flavor attitudes, not dominate them, and it should be a servant to individual roles, not define them. For example, one CIO (Chief Information Officer) of an airline attended his first executive meeting where the decision needed to be made to buy or lease three new aircraft. When the CEO went around the table and asked the CIO for his opinion, he said that he was a technologist and therefore had nothing to contribute. The CEO smiled warmly to soften the message and said: "Everything this team does concerns you. Next time, I would like you to have an opinion on each topic under discussion. After all, you bring a unique perspective to the table." The CIO realized that his knowledge and experience allowed him to view every element of the business uniquely and began to take an interest in every aspect of the company. Ten years later, he became the CEO.

There is no time or space in the C-Suite to be functional partisans. That most executives come from a functional background is clear, but when they hit the C-Suite, everything changes. They have teams to manage their functions, so they should let them manage. The executive's job is to find out what is happening in the world, think and filter, model their thoughts, communicate, guide, motivate, support, and reinforce their people. We started the chapter with words like powerful, influential, experienced, and responsible. These words still hold true, but their meaning has changed: C-Suite executives are powerful, not because of the control they have, but because they have the power to help others see the things they see and act accordingly. They are influential, not because everyone follows them blindly, but because they influence their organization's worldview and its place in that world. They are experienced, but not dogmatic. Instead, they allow their experience to flavor their thinking, to serve themselves and others, and to help others because of what they have observed, encountered or undergone. Finally, they are responsible for how their organization functions and not how their department performs. They are also responsible in that they are ethical, moral, and humane.

OUTSIDE-IN THINKING

The subtitle of this book is: "Evolving your executive team to meet today's challenges," and the first part describes some of the challenges such as education, the digital world, different generations and how they work, and continually changing customer expectations. I've also talked about how the emphasis of business economics has moved from the supply side (where economies of scale, organization, processes, functions, and command and control are regarded as being important), to the demand side (where network effects, ecosystems, customer focus, and leadership dominate executives' thinking). This shift in emphasis is profound and requires an equally profound change in how the C-Suite operates and what its role is. I've already talked about the need to provide leadership rather than management, but it is the nature of leadership needed that changes profoundly.

In summary, C-Suite executives need to devolve all management activities to their people and to reposition their leadership focus from inside-out to outside-in.

Inside-out thinking is where an executive looks at what products or services his or her company sells and finds customers who will buy it. Outside-in thinking requires them to look at what customers need and find ways to meet those needs. It's a shift from supply-side to demand-side thinking, and it dramatically changes the role of the C-Suite.

Inside-out thinking starts inside the organization and views the outside environment as a map to be navigated. Inside questions begin with who we are and what do we do. Many companies have failed by getting the answer to this question wrong. Blockbuster placed itself in the video rental business, rather than the home entertainment business, and was unable to transition to digital, even though they were approached by Netflix. Borders an international book and music retailer failed to adopt digital platforms. Polaroid and Kodak didn't go digital and died. The central theme here was that these companies did not see their industry as more than their product and could not adjust their business model to accommodate changes. Another inside question is, "Who are our customers, and what will they buy from us?" Again, this is an issue because this question defines customers in terms of who we are, not who they are. The Blockbuster example is a classic example, defining customers in terms of video rental and ignoring all possible digital customers, which is sad, because digital customers occur all over the world, not just near Blockbuster stores. A final inside-out question concerns competitors. Defining your competitors in terms of your products is a mistake. PC manufacturers who compete with other PC manufacturers ignore competitive threats from smartphones, tablets, and the cloud. Surprisingly, Microsoft, despite being successful, has ignored Web TV, e-books, smartphones, and tablets (even though there is an MS operating system for tablets and smartphones, it came so late that they have virtually no market share). Sears did not recognize that their competition was online. The danger of inside-out thinking is that it defines the world in your terms, which blinds you to the product, customer, and competitive opportunities. A further risk is that you think that you see your business as the center of your own universe, rather than a component of an ecosystem.

Outside-in thinking starts with … drum roll … looking outside. What changes in society, or the economy, are creating a need or problem? Notice that you haven't asked who your customers are. But you have identified needs and potential requirements. You have to also look internally, not at your products, but at what your capabilities are. For example, if we look at Tesla electric cars, we see that they looked at the environment and society and recognized a nascent need for non-internal combustion vehicles. They define themselves as a technology company (their capabilities), which manufactures automobiles. In 2018 they made 245,000 cars and had a revenue of $21 billion. Not bad for a company that started when GM recalled its EV1 electric cars and destroyed them. Because Tesla defines themselves as a technology company, their strategy is based on technology adoption life-cycles (not automobile life-cycles), and they also sell batteries and solar panels. Because they see themselves in an ecosystem, they partner with automobile manufacturers, battery makers, charging locations such as Airbnb, and an insurance company that provided cover specifically for electric vehicles. Tesla has had problems with manufacturing, but its customers are passionate about the cars. However, it took until early 2019 to make a profit. Whether the company succeeds or not, doesn't detract from their outside-in strategy.

SCANNING THE ENVIRONMENT

The C-Suite should be scanning developments in society, the economy and industry, and regulations. They should also track customer requirements, technology, competitors, suppliers, and the business environment. The first set of scanned elements affects the entire business domain, while the second set affects the organization's ecosystem. Political and environmental developments should also be scanned.

An example of societal scanning includes the trend of declining birth rates in many countries, so Johnson & Johnson repositioned their baby shampoo and baby oil for the adult female market. PepsiCo realized that people were becoming more focused on health and wellness and repositioned themselves as a nutritional company. An example of business environmental scanning is the recognition that the rate of change in technology is increasing, and that product life-cycles are compressing. This means that if you take too long to develop a product, it may be obsolete by the time it is launched. This has led to the concept of MVP (minimum viable product) development. Some companies produce the minimum number of functions in a new product then test it on a few customers. If customers like it, they continue developing the product further. In this way, expenditure on new products is minimized. Also, if customers want changes, the product can evolve in the right direction. Both MVP development and the adoption of agile development have arisen as a result of business trends and customer scanning.

Because these trends are increasing in their rate of change, identifying those that represent opportunities or threats to the organization is a critical role. An associated discipline with scanning is scenario planning. Scenario planning is where executives examine the significant drivers that will affect their organization. That's where scanning comes in – choosing the right drivers. For instance, using the above example, two drivers might be product lifecycles and technology change. Xerox used scenario planning to anticipate the convergence of printers and copiers by looking at the drivers behind paper-based and digital information. American Express used scenario planning to foresee the replacement of traveler's cheques with cards. And in a little known example, Anglo American used scenario planning to outline a high-road/low-road scenario for apartheid South Africa in 1986. They embarked on a free roadshow across the country to all citizens who would listen. Such was their success that the apartheid government called them in to help plan how the country could follow the high-road scenario. In 1990, the ANC (the opposition movement) was unbanned, freeing the way for free elections in 1994. Scenario planning is not about predicting the future. It predicts four possible futures, depending on how the drivers pan out over time. The C-Suite then tracks what is happening with the drivers and can plan for the more probable scenario. The benefits of scenario planning include systems thinking, risk management, and the optimal allocation of resources. Systems thinking examines elements as they relate to each other. Scenario planning is a simple process, but the thought required can be difficult.

The C-Suite needs to think and apply filters for their organization. This doesn't mean that others in the organization shouldn't think, they should, but the focus of C-Suite thinking makes the difference. In Chapter 2, I talked about divergent and convergent thinking. Divergent thought creates new opportunities and options, and convergent thought solves problems and involves the application of judgment. I try to use a seven-step process when considering an issue:

1. Define the scope and boundaries of the issue: This is already a filtering process. If we try to solve everything at once, we'll probably not get a compelling plan of action. Successful executives think about a few problems at one time – they actively narrow their attention to significant issues.

2. Think divergently about the defined issue: This is brainstorming – coming up with as many ideas and possibilities as possible. Stay in divergent mode – most brainstorming is ineffective as participants move into judgment mode too quickly (some never leave judgment mode).

3. Apply convergent thinking: Only after exhausting the options, should you start to think about what is possible. The aim of this step is not to find one possible path. Instead, it is to identify a few (5–7) possible solutions. In other words, we are still keeping the door open for several options.

4. List the possible options: Some will require more work and resources, and some may need other events to happen or elements to be put in place but keep them in the frame.

5. Apply divergent thinking to each option: This is where we think about each option separately and apply "what if" thoughts. For example, if an alternative is to open several new branches in a new country, someone might say: "What if we partner with someone who already has a branch network in that country?"

6. Converge for each option: Use insightful judgment for each alternative solution. In some cases, this might require more information to develop insight. In the above example of partnering with someone, a little research might be needed before one can accept or discount the idea.

7. Prioritize the alternatives: This is especially true of scenario planning as some options might work better in different scenarios. Even if one selects a single option, the others might provide a backup plan if things go wrong.

MODELING THE THINKING

Once a plan of action is settled, the C-Suite needs to model their thinking. The first element is a mental model, which is an internal symbolic representation of external reality. This model simplifies reality and helps in understanding, reasoning, and decision-making. It also assists the executive in communicating their opinions and worldviews. There are some caveats to understand about any model, mental or otherwise. They are a representation of reality, not reality – the map is not the territory, as Alfred Korzybski said years ago. And because a model is a representation, it reduces reality to manageable levels, is a simplification reality, and is a filtered artifact. If a map were to represent the territory with absolute fidelity, it would have to be the exact size of the territory and wouldn't be a representation or model anymore. Because a model is a simplification, it can appear to be a misrepresentation of how complex things really are. And it is a filtered artifact because it depends on the mindset and beliefs of the person who created it, and, as a result, may not be understood by someone with a different mindset.

Nevertheless, mental models are useful and essential to us as people, and to executives in particular. Especially when the executive understands the process of creating them, the benefits and limitations associated with them, and the role that models play in his organization. They help us understand the world, develop concepts and ideas about how things work, recognize deficiencies and opportunities in our thinking, navigate to a new place or reality, and finally, to communicate better. And to express our mental model thinking, we usually have to make it visible to others.

A visual model is usually a depiction of our mental model or a network of models. For the C-Suite, the purpose of a visual model is to make the thinking and direction involved in a particular course of action available to others. Simple visual models are a hierarchical chart or a process diagram. They show linkages and relationships between concepts. A typical model to consider is the business model – usually, it covers how an organization will make money by providing a value proposition (what people will buy), underpinned by its capabilities, partners, ecosystem, and critical resources.

But let's take a more straightforward example. We want to explain how we want the company to operate in the future because the current hierarchy and functional departments are inefficient, costly, and create silos. After discussions and thinking, backed by research, we believe that there are two primary foci that the organization should have: Customer experience, and internal culture and capabilities. We can write a chapter on each of these, but that's not the purpose in this example. We also have three stages for each of these foci: Strategy and planning (thinking), transformation (change), and delivery (doing). The simple model could be depicted as shown in Figure 12.1:

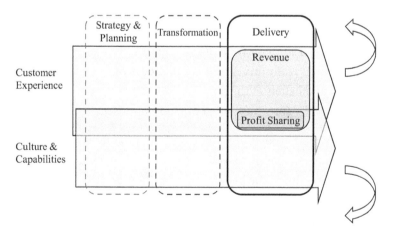

Figure 12.1 Simple model of the new organization

In this example of a model to explain how we want the company to operate in the future, I've made some symbolic decisions. Firstly, the customer experience and culture/capabilities foci are represented as overlapping arrows to show that we are moving forward to deliver and that even once we have achieved that, we want the arrows to circle back to the strategy phase again. I've made the strategy and transformation phases dotted lines because I want people to understand that this is not the main activity of the business, which is also why I've made the delivery phase a bold black outline because that's how we make our revenue. I've even inserted a "profit sharing" box to show that at the interception of delivery, revenue, culture, and capabilities are where individuals stand to gain from the company's performance. On examination, this appears to be a simple model, but it covers most of what this company does. It demonstrates a change in focus, a commitment to reducing silo thinking, a new form of organization, a commitment to thinking and changing, and that delivery and revenue is essential to the future of the company. The curved arrows at the right of the model indicate that we want to learn from what and how we deliver, and that what we learn must be thought about and drive change in the organization. So, a model can tell a thousand stories, and that's what we move on to next – communication.

COMMUNICATING

Dr. Gordon Coates said: "Communication is one of the most important things we ever do. It is the interpersonal equivalent of breathing."[1] And if it is essential to interaction, why are some people bad at it. Possibly, as Coates suggests, it is because, like breathing, we take communication for granted. I mean we all communicate, don't we? However, "communication" has two elements to its definition. The first element comes from the Latin word "communicare," which means "to share" or "make common," and the second component is related to information and meaning. So, communication is about sharing information and common meaning. And that's where the problem creeps in. Sharing is not transmitting, and common meaning is uncommon in many organizations, which is why C-Suite executives need to understand and master communication more than any other team in the organization. Transmission is a one-directional process, while sharing is bi-directional – to communicate, you must listen as well. Listening is more than nodding politely until you get to speak. As Charlene Headlee[2] says, it's much harder to listen than to talk. Talking means you're in control, requires effort, and often is about ego. Some of the techniques that Headlee recommends are: Don't multitask – if you're listening, then listen; Go with the flow – ideas and thoughts will flow into your head, let them go, and listen to the speaker; and, if you don't know, say you don't know. Common meaning requires everyone in the organization to understand the mental models of executives and to buy into them.

Coates says that communication should be a two-way process, but that delivering advice or instructions is also communication, which, to my mind, is flawed. However, too many executives practice one-way communication, then wonder why no-one buys into their message. By the way, this book is one-way communication, like a message in a bottle, but I hope that readers will complete the two-way loop by contributing to the blog page at www.terrygrey.com, a website set up expressly for this book. I look forward to reading your feedback and ideas. But back to the basics of communication. There are thousands of books, videos, and courses on communication, so I'll only touch on some aspects, as they apply to the C-Suite.

Communication consists of three components: The sender, the channel, and the receiver. For our purposes, the C-Suite senders include all executives on the team. The issue here, which I've discussed before, is the unity of the messages sent. If the C-Suite is sending out discordant messages, the receivers will probably reflect that discord. However, there are several styles in which executives communicate, depending upon who they are.

The channels through which the C-Suite communicates should differ according to the message. Some people have a visual style. They use words with a visual context. They use phrases like: "It *looks* to me …, My *view* is …, I *see* …, *Imagine* if …," and so on. Auditory phrases include: "Clear as a *bell*, I like the *sound* of …, *Report* …," and "*inquire* into …" There is also the tactile style: "Gut *feeling*, *touch* base, keep in *contact*," and the closely related kinesthetic style: "*Pull* some strings, *start* from scratch, and *firm* foundation." Here's the point (which is a tactile word): The communication styles of executives will be different, and the C-Suite should try to ensure that the style matches the message. If you're talking about the future, an executive with a visual style will send signals which are coherent with the message: "We see our vision as follows." Match transformation styles with transformation messages, as the style is about movement, content that could spark emotions with the tactile style as it is about feelings, and fact-finding with auditory. Clearly, for executives and messages, one style cannot be used exclusively, but it's a useful trick to match the dominant style of the executive with the core of the message.

Channels in organizations can be simple face-to-face, or broadcast like email, video, posters, or engaging through meetings and workshops, or even passive like portals and websites. The type of message you send should dictate the medium. Face-to-face communication should be the vehicle for personal communication concerning performance, remuneration, and job movements. One should engage and involve people when we are looking for them to commit to a course of action. This is because a dialogue, rather than a one-way message is required. People will not buy in or commit to an initiative unless they can question and delve deeper into the thinking behind the action because this affects them on a personal level. Broadcasts are one-way messages and should be reserved for general, non-contentious messages. Which brings us to how executives should order their messages. If the organization is embarking on any course which will affect people, then those people need to receive the information as follows: First, they should be made aware that something is about to happen. It is risky to give people information without them being aware of the context into which they should put it. It is equally risky to make people aware that something will happen unless the data supporting it is available. So one should broadcast "awareness" messages, alerting people to an initiative or event and directing them to a passive channel, like a portal, for more information.

The next step is to ensure that the information is more than passively accepted because many, if not most people, in large corporates are passive. (We've covered the reasons in Chapter 6.) So now broadcast channels can be used to transmit core information, with directions to more information and where to find it. The third step is to engage teams and individuals using workshops and forums. Some companies can run workshops with hundreds of people, but this is difficult and expensive to do. Usually, the workshops will involve teams or hierarchical layers. Alternatively, an online portal can act as a virtual workshop. The emphasis here is to allow multi-directional dialog. The aim is to enable people to commit themselves to the concept, or initiative, and to provide their own inputs, either as it affects them locally, or even company-wide.

The final step in communicating a concept or initiative is operational communication. These are manuals, wiki applications, policies, and procedures. The ideal operational communication is one that has real feedback loops in it. I use the phrase "real feedback loops" very deliberately. I use the word "real" because many organizations include: "Contact Us," "We want to hear from you," and bots that ask "Do you want to chat?" without any commitment to listening, acting, or changing their products or processes (or even their attitudes to customers and suppliers). Feedback is essential today – from all stakeholders: customers, suppliers, staff, and the community. In a digital world, feedback is probably the most powerful tool in the improvement, innovation, and design tool of any organization. And finally, I use the word "loop" because it is a continuous process. A feedback loop is part of a system in which some portion of the system's output is used as input for future operations. That's the general definition, but let's unpack it in an organizational context. We've already talked about business ecosystems in Chapter 10. Feedback loops are the central mechanism for driving the ecosystem, otherwise it would be a static field of components, not related and not developing or evolving. Customers and staff are components of the system, and their feedback is critical to the survival and growth of the organization. There is always feedback – saying nothing is a message, perhaps a more powerful one than saying something. Executives who believe that "no news is good news" are living in the wrong business reality. You always want feedback, both good and bad.

In summary, to communicate well, one needs to make people aware of an issue first, then provide them with information about the issue. Only then can one move to engage people, to gain commitment and feedback, and then operationalize the messages. Feedback remains an essential part of every step in the communication process. We can modify the old saying: "If a tree falls in a forest, and no-one hears it, does it make a noise?" to "If someone sends a message and no-one receives it, is it still communication?" The answer is no (for the communication, not the tree).

So, we need a receiver of a message as much as we need a sender. And the meaning of a message will be what the receiver assigns to it, not what the sender necessarily has in mind. The challenge of communication is to get the sender's meaning as close to the received meaning as possible. To do that, we need to understand the receiver, his or her mental models, beliefs, and experiences. The problem often is that executives send out messages consistent with their own opinions and, as a result, the meaning will be lost or misinterpreted by the receiver, which negates the purpose of the sender communicating in the first place. There can be difficulties on the receiver side as well. The receiver can also not receive the message correctly if they do not have the conceptual vocabulary of the sender – this is why models and the awareness phase of communication are critical. The receiver may be intimidated or threatened by the sender of the message and won't concentrate or ask clarification questions. The receiver may not be interested or even too busy to pay attention to the message, or the receiver is close-minded or merely unmotivated.

There can be problems with the sender, the channels, and the receiver, which makes one wonder if effective communication can occur at all. The answer lies, of course, in feedback: With real feedback, it is possible to align meaning, receive criticisms or ideas, refine the message, extend the discussion, change channels, interpret non-verbal and verbal cues … the list goes on. It is probably fair to say that without feedback, communication doesn't exist. It does, of course, but it may just be a tree falling in a forest.

GUIDING, INFLUENCING, AND MOTIVATING

I t turns out that I wrote a whole chapter on this section, but much of it
was mundane and could be studied in many texts, videos, and courses.
So, I decided not to repeat material that is freely available elsewhere, and to
write only a few paragraphs that relate to this book.

I've covered the concept of leadership being MAST (meaning, attention,
self, and trust). Scanning and modeling include, to some extent, the
management of meaning. Modeling and communication deal with some
aspects of the management of attention. Self and trust are really to do
with how the executive understands him- or herself and will be covered in
Chapter 13. However, guidance, influence, and motivation are dependent
on self and trust, as much as the subject of the guidance itself.

Guidance is an interesting word, in that in the organizational context,
it means leadership, advice, and focus. In a military sense (guidance
systems), it involves altering the speed and direction of something in
response to controls. We can take from that definition and use it in an
organizational sense – mostly about the altering, direction, and control.
So for our purposes, guidance involves advising others to focus on a
particular concept or initiative, thus altering their perceptions, behaviors,
and actions. Control, in this sense, I choose to mean feedback loops,
rather than command. We've covered focusing on a particular concept in
meaning and attention management. The guidance is required when more
clarity is needed or the receiver's interpretation differs from the sender's.
Alternatively, guidance is necessary when a staff member has a problem,
challenge, or opportunity – "What should I do?" Here the executive should
filter his or her responses through the organization's vision, strategy,
culture, and capabilities, as well as through the available mental models.

Influence, when you read the texts, is all about understanding the person
you want to influence, creating trust, and establishing a sense of urgency,
and so on. I would prefer to put influence and motivation together and

take it from the other angle. When Michael Porter said: "Everything sends a message," I imagine that being influenced and motivated is one of the primary effects of the message that was sent. Both influence and motivation can be positive or negative. We're hoping for positive influence and motivation, naturally, but negative influence can cause people to often imitate the executive's behavior. Negative motivation results in deteriorating performance, outputs, attitudes, and culture. For the C-Suite, I believe that positive influence and motivation are the results of the beliefs, attitudes, behaviors, and actions of executives, and that the negative effects are exacerbated by power-games, command and control mindsets, hierarchy, bureaucracy, ego, self-importance … pretty much everything that many corporates do right now. It's one of the reasons I am writing this book.

NOTES

1 Gordon T Coates, *Notes on Communication: A Few Thoughts about the Way We Interact with the People We Meet*. Free e-book from www.wanterfall.com, 2009.
2 Celeste Headlee, *10 Ways to have a Better Conversation*, TEDx CreativeCoast, March 8, 2016. www.youtube.com/watch?v=R1vskiVDwl4, [Accessed August 2019].

CHAPTER THIRTEEN
The skills and attributes of the C-Suite

The skills of the C-Suite will depend on their roles. They will also depend on the organization's mission and ecosystem. There is an assumption that the C-Suite is a static unit, and this premise should also be tested. If people are paid for their performance and not their title and time, perhaps the C-Suite is a flexible concept, growing and shrinking as needs require. We'll deal with the evolved C-Suite in Chapter 15, but for now, let's look at what executives need to be skilled at.

THE INTELLIGENCE OF THE C-SUITE

There are several abilities that executives need to master as a result of being in the C-Suite. Their intelligence should be more than those catered for by the education system. They need to be able to navigate through complexity, demonstrate wisdom, and should offer leadership skills.

Schools and universities mainly cater for linguistic and logical-mathematical intelligence. There are several other forms of intelligence that are not explicitly accommodated, although universities do touch on them: Spatial, intrapersonal, interpersonal, and creative intelligence. In a business environment, spatial intelligence is the ability to visualize things and the ability to see things as models of reality. We covered scanning and modeling in Chapter 12, and the ability to do so is an essential component of the executive's skillset.

Intrapersonal intelligence is the ability to understand yourself, it requires self-awareness and introspection. Executives with intrapersonal understanding, are self-motivated, independent without being rebels, goal-oriented for the entire organization, confident without being arrogant, positive while excluding hubris, and skilled at self-reflection. Albert Einstein used to do much of his thinking during long walks. At this time, he thought critically and formulated his theories about the cosmos and the way the universe works. He spent lots of time alone and operated independently. Intrapersonal (intra – within) intelligence is the intelligence of the self. It strengthens the executive's ability to decipher and analyze their reasons for acting, their wants and needs, understand their thoughts, and identify and manage their feelings. People with this intelligence are often introverted, which may conflict with an executive's leadership mandate and with the requirement for interpersonal intelligence, a component of which is extroversion. The skill can be taught by taking time to meditate and to write down one's ideas.

Executives with interpersonal intelligence are good with people and thrive on social interaction. They are extroverted, empathetic, counsel others, and listen well. Being empathetic means they identify with the moods, feelings, and motivations of others. They are skilled in understanding and managing relationships and negotiating conflict. They can discern the intentions and desires of others, even if they have been hidden. They like being with people, working in a team, and enjoy social interactions. They encourage dialog and discussions with enthusiasm. They are inclusive of others and are experts at collaboration. Others come to them for advice, help, and comfort. They are natural leaders.

Executives with spatial intelligence are aware of their surroundings, can visualize concepts, and use colors, shapes, and symbolic representations to illustrate their thinking. They like puzzles and complexity. They can simplify challenging ideas into mental models that they can represent to others in a way that they understand. Spatial intelligence involves visiual, abstract, and analytical abilities. These abilities allow the executive to recognize objects or concepts, understand their relationships to other components, and represent the structure of their construct to others.

While Howard Gardner was the creator of the nine intelligences, he did not include creative intelligence as one of these. However, Bruce Nussbaum wrote a book called "Creative Intelligence,"[1] in which he talks about people who can operate in areas of uncertainty. While uncertainty makes many people uncomfortable or even fearful, creative people revel in ambiguity. They are, Nussbaum says, wanderers, who think outside the organization and can blend disparate ideas into a cohesive whole. They are, as Claus Møller[2] says, people who have: "… the ability to go beyond the existing to create novel and interesting ideas." Møller says that creative people question assumptions, expect and allow mistakes, actively define and redefine problems, and take sensible risks. Moreover, they allow others to be creative, reward creativity, seek out role models, and understand the obstacles that creative people face.

If the C-Suite needs the intelligences of linguistics, logic, self-understanding, interpersonal skills, and spatial and creative abilities, it is unlikely to find these in one person. That's why the C-Suite must be a team, which complements each other's skills and intelligence, and, importantly, knows when one member or group should dominate activities. Indeed, an individual's C-Suite skills and intelligence contradicts and often opposes another's. They should be cross-paired with each other to produce an effect more significant than the individual.

DEALING WITH COMPLEXITY

If there's one primary dimension in being a C-Suite executive, it is complexity. Complex systems are composed of many interconnected parts, compounded by constant movement and change, very often developing an unpredictable character. To make matters worse, very few people can agree on the interpretation of complex components. "Complex" is not the same as "complicated." A watch or motorcar is complicated, but they operate in the same way, every time. A complex system will behave differently depending on the environment in which it occurs and the inputs which it receives. And while business is complicated, its changing nature and unpredictability define it as a complex system. When one researches complex systems, one finds that they cannot be controlled or overpowered and that the only sensible approach is self-organization, which is why Chapter 14 is mostly about self-managed teams and complex-adaptive systems.

However, the skill of dealing with complexity is an adjunct to self-organization, which executives must master. Ralph Stacey[3] developed

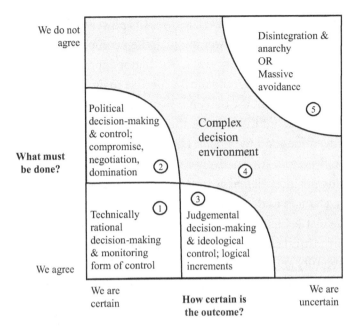

Figure 13.1 Stacey's model for complexity

an instructive model that helps executives view complexity and complex decisions in an organizational context. He considers two factors: Whether executives and experts agree on what must be done and how certain we can be. He draws two axes and represents the organizational environment as shown in Figure 13.1:

I've altered some of the words that Stacey uses, but the essence is the same. Let's look at the five scenarios that Stacey considers:

1. Where we all agree on what must be done and we are certain that the outcome will be reached if we act in a certain way, then we can make purely rational decisions and merely monitor the progress. In most organizations, these decisions are standardized, procedural, and delegated to those closest to the activity concerned.
2. When the team is certain about what will happen but disagree on what must be done to give effect to the desired outcome, then politics enter into the equation. If a member of the team is politically

powerful (usually the CEO), he uses his power to force the decision. However, if political power is equal, then compromise, negotiations or dominant behavior prevails. The better approach would be to allow the person with the most expertise to dominate.

3. Uncertainty about the outcome (we're not sure what we want), but agreement about the fact that there must be some outcome, results in the need for good judgment. Here, again, the person with expertise should prevail. Alternatively, as many organizations are now doing, opting for incremental advances, with regular checks and, if necessary, changes in direction are a method of approaching the issue.

4. In a volatile business environment, with rapid shifts in technology, many critical choices fall into the complex decision environment. Ambiguity and lack of information will need to be factored into our decisions because many factors are beyond our control. Linear decisions (like a five-year plan) cannot work. Scenario planning is an attractive option, especially if the organization has an ineffective self-correcting mechanism. Cause-and-effect dynamics mean that there should be constant monitoring of the environment, and there should be an open-minded approach to changing the decision and its parameters if the monitoring shows that initial assumptions are wrong.

5. Where the outcome is too uncertain, and few people agree on what to do, there tend to be two typical responses, aligned with the "fight or flight" reflex. Everyone can try to do something, or some people will do nothing. As Stacey says, it results in anarchy or avoidance. Scenario planning can again help, but the issue of agreement on drivers of the scenario comes up. Another option is to "divide and conquer" (not the team, but the problem). By defining the broad components of the problem, one can then delimit the scope of just that problem. This could result in the decision moving into the complex space rather than staying in what Stacey calls the "chaos zone."

The above figure deals with cognitive complexity (how people think in complex situations), but behavioral complexity is also a factor in C-Suite executives. Behavioral complexity relates to how people adapt to other people, groups or structures. Adaptability in ambiguous social and organizational circumstances is the key here. It requires constant appraisal and reappraisal of conditions and relationships.

THE WISDOM OF THE C-SUITE

Executive wisdom is complex. It involves the executive's thoughts, behavior, emotions, and history. It requires care and circumspection, observation and sensing, rationality and irrationality, and practicality and spirituality.

There is considerable pressure on executives given the intelligence they must have, the ability to deal with complexity, and the conditions in which they must lead and work. To cope with this pressure and be wise at the same time requires a spiritual and mental acuity that is difficult to achieve.[4] Spirituality comes into the equation because wisdom needs executives to be rational, but also to accept, or even encourage, non-rational and subjective opinions and behaviors in others and themselves. They know that sensory and intuitive views are useful elements of decision-making. Wise executives are careful observers and use their wisdom to evaluate the salience (importance of something being considered) and the truth of what they see. They also act on what they believe to be worthwhile to more than themselves and for an elevated cause – it is right, sound, and appropriate.

A wise executive acknowledges that decision-making is dependent and rarely involves the application of absolute rules. Therefore, they need to be practical, and while knowing the rules, they should know when and how to apply them in ambiguous circumstances. They are circumspect in their wisdom, relying on their own knowledge, experience, and background. Part of this practicality involves being able to articulate to others how and why they use their judgment and decision-making. They should be guided by their inner sense of right and wrong, but as seen in many cases, they are not. As Aristotle says, people should do: "what one does, just because one sees those actions as noble and worthwhile."

There are a lot of words above like: "elevated, right, sound, and appropriate," which brings us to the question of corporate and business ethics. Ethics involves decisions and actions taken under controversial or questionable circumstances, including governance, discrimination, social responsibility, bribery, and regulatory responsibilities. The law often guides business ethics, and regulations such as the Sarbanes Oxley Act specifically focus on corporate accountability, responsibility, and transparency. Nevertheless, many executives are faced with ethical decisions in other areas.

Sadly, cases such as Enron and Worldcom show that many executives are not ethical. Enron kept huge debts off their balance sheet to make their financials look good – so good that Fortune Magazine named them "America's most innovative company" for six years in a row. Their innovation with debt, cost their shareholders $74 billion and cost thousands of jobs. Enron executives were jailed, the company filed for bankruptcy, and Arthur Andersen was found guilty of fudging Enron's accounts. Worldcom inflated its assets by $11 billion and internal fraud amounting to $3.8 billion was uncovered. Thirty thousand jobs were lost and investors lost $180 billion. The company went bankrupt and executives were fired or went to jail. The list goes on, so ethics and fraud are a real issue in business.

Business ethics is more than morality. Companies need to be competitive, and in doing so will often shave corners. So ethics is more than right and wrong, it is also about the trust of consumers and investors and the regulations that must be adhered to. Poor business ethics include marketing goods as healthy when they are not. For example, many companies list their sugar-free ingredients as "high fructose corn syrup" and "maltodextrin," both of which are forms of sugar. Another example of poor business ethics would be a company that skimps on quality control because they have a deadline. We're ignoring the elephant in the room when it comes to ethics – internal combustion engines which are polluting the planet, the meat industry which does worse, fast food, sugar, cigarettes, and many other sectors which know what they sell is wrong for people and the planet but continue to do so. Bad business ethics are when a company or an executive knowingly ignores the best interests of its employees, customers, society or the environment.

Positive ethics exist as well: The "fair trade" movement where fair prices are paid for goods, particularly in developing countries; ethical farming practices; green corporate buildings; and so on. Sadly, these practices are far outweighed by businesses with profit motives that ignore the responsibilities they should ethically adopt. Ben Teehankee,[5] a business ethics professor, presents arguments that his audiences raise when he lectures on business ethics. Firstly, ethics depend on values that are formed during early childhood and cannot be changed. Teehankee highlights several companies that have practiced bad ethics, but given facts, education, and reflection have changed their practices. Secondly, people argue that ethical leadership comes from the top, and those without power can do nothing. Again, Teehankee refers to whistleblowers, of which there are many examples, or people who quietly do the right thing, in spite of what their leaders do. Finally, some contend that companies cannot be profitable and ethical as well. The United Kingdom's Institute of Business Ethics studied 350 FTSE firms who had an "ethical culture" and found that they outperformed companies who made no such claims.

Shane Green, the author of "Culture Hacker,"[6] said: "In today's transparent social-media-driven world, senior executives, especially those with a high profile, will be tested and called to task over their morals and ethics in how they do business." Doing business in a digital world, where society is continuously connected, and individuals can post observations and comments anywhere, means that poor ethical behaviors will surface quickly and be widely distributed. This is not a threat. Instead, it is a recognition of the fact that an executive's practices and actions are more visible than ever before. Executives should examine their values and bring them to the workplace. They should be secure in making them visible to their organization. They should associate with and hire people with similar values. And they should promote transparency. They should strive for fairness and be aware of their own, and others', biases. Finally, they should talk about ethics. And if your values don't equate to ethical work practices, be aware of Shane Green's quote above.

DIGITAL FLUENCY

As the pace of change in digital business accelerates, companies are succeeding or failing based on their digital acuity. Most organizations have technical people who know what needs to be done and are enthusiastic about getting their point across. In my experience, many of these techies are not good communicators. They use jargon or lose sight of the business reasoning needed to get an idea across. The fault is mostly theirs, and I have spent considerable time translating tech-speak into language that makes sense to business executives. But there is some fault to be found with executives as well. I've heard this comment hundreds of times from an executive: "I don't know much about technology, but I know it costs too much." Many executives don't know much about technology because of their ego – they don't want to ask questions that appear stupid. Others see technology as an arcane discipline, with its own language and culture, and hold up their hands when approached by one of the high-priests of technology. Some recall the past experience with tech disasters and distrust all technology, even though it has moved on since their exposure to it. Finally, and I call these "silver bullet" executives, believe that technology will solve everything, easily and quickly. Whatever the reason, their reluctance to engage with technology could hold their company back at best or cause it to fail at worst.

Digital fluency is not the same as digital expertise – that's what the technologists are for. But modern executives must understand enough about technology, firstly, not to have the wool pulled over their eyes, and secondly, to make sound decisions about technology and its place in the business model. Resolving the "wool over the eyes" is easy, but it does require a little humility. Years ago, I was sitting in the office of my tech manager, whom I regarded as one of the most tech-savvy people I had met. His systems manager was explaining some aspects of a problem they were having, and my tech manager stopped him and said: "Louis, I have no idea what you're talking about." It was at that moment that I realized that the tech field is so vast and complicated that no-one can know it all, or even a substantial portion of it. So I adopted a simple strategy: When a techie wasn't making sense to me, I said so and asked him to explain again in business terms. If he couldn't, I asked him to come back when he could explain so that I could understand. I still don't know much about technology, but I am digitally fluent. My tech team became business fluent.

Digital fluency requires that executives are aware of technology trends and what they mean for the business. It is not difficult. All you need is to be able to search the internet intelligently. A simple search entitled: "Latest technologies that will affect business" will show a list of search results that include artificial intelligence, the internet of things (IoT), and cybersecurity, among a relatively short list. Then another search, "What does artificial intelligence mean for business?" will return a list of articles covering AI for business. And that's it. A morning's work will get you up to speed – as far as you need to go – in the latest technology trends. Don't get involved in the technical details – you want fluency, not expertise. Another search on "How is the way we do business changing?" will generate articles like "15 trends that change the way you do business," and "6 ways business is changing." Be aware that several search results will be about how technology is changing business, because, well, it is. A quiet day spent searching for technology and business or commerce, the environment or whatever your business does and you will be fluent with the latest trends in your particular area. I did a search for "How is technology changing government?" just to see what the results would be and came up with several useful insights.

Digital fluency also requires that you keep abreast of technologies that may help your organization perform better. Again, the "search on a phrase" technique works well. For instance, searching on "how technology changes the way we work" will return many useful results. One can do such searches for "strategy planning software" or "process optimization software" and you will become fluent in that topic quickly. Notice that I changed from "technology" to "software" – you could use "solutions" or "tools" – because I am looking for tools that will help aspects of my business improve. Also, once you have found a tool or trend that you would like to know more about, I find Wikipedia is a good source of background, history, and overviews. One thing you should look at, though, is something called Enterprise Architecture tools. Enterprise Architecture (EA) is one of the arcane technology disciplines that has been around since the 1980s, but in the last two years, it has changed dramatically. While the "old" version was used by corporate technologists to plan how their technology would meet business needs, the "new" version is a business planning, simulation, and decision support tool. You can model your business, your customer journeys, your capabilities, processes, and technologies. The useful thing here is that you can then conduct "what if" analyses on your model, to assess the effects and financial implications of any move that you might be contemplating. Sort of like scenario planning on an ongoing basis, but it's available to everyone in the organization – most EA tools are regarded as the single version of the truth.

Digital fluency in business ecosystems is a little different. Executives should know how their organization's technology interfaces and works with other players in the ecosystem. In past times, companies protected their technology and kept technologically to themselves, but as we've said before, your organization is part of a business ecosystem. It makes sense to understand how the technology works so that you can take advantage of efficiencies, economies of scale, and complimentary services. The first technical advantage is in allowing ecosystem participants to interact with each other. This can be done using ecosystem-specific collaboration tools, which confines access to ecosystem players. As with everything technological, a search on "business collaboration tools" will give you your options. Customers, however, should also have access to the ecosystem on an open platform, like Facebook or Twitter. This can be branded and managed to reflect the ecosystem's offerings. One of the issues with open platforms is response times. Customers expect replies to their queries, complaints, and comments within 60 minutes, as discussed in Chapter 9, so some effort must be made to monitor and manage the customer interface for the ecosystem.

Business ecosystems also share data which should be standardized and normalized. Normalization involves structuring and managing data so there is no duplication, there is version control, and the data that is available to the ecosystem is current and correct. (This is a big deal. It's complicated to do and is essential to effective operations.) Similarly, the technology used by ecosystem members should be standardized as far as possible. This is less of an issue since most technology manufacturers adopt standards that do this already, but occasionally, one company might be using proprietary software, which makes it difficult to interact with others. Several vendors specialize in supplying and managing business ecosystem software, like SAP, Oracle, Microsoft – all the big software houses. There are industry-specific platforms that link suppliers in a customer journey, like travel sites, taxi-hailing services, banking – pick an industry. Finally, some services that integrate multiple organizations around a specific function like customers (Salesforce), processes (Slack), and many EA tools cater for operations within an ecosystem.

MANAGING CHANGE

If an organization hasn't moved to self-managed teams and a complex adaptive system approach, then they will need to manage change. This requires executives to prepare their teams and the organization through significant changes. However, Ed Schein, author of "Humble Leadership," says: "If you're talking about people who have been anointed – they're presidents, they're CEOs, they're supposed to be leaders – then that's one reason … (transformation) … is being held back."[7] If leaders are appointed and are not natural leaders, change will be difficult, if not impossible. Change management tries to gain commitment from people so that they lead the change themselves. Executives must map out the changes that are coming, identify how they will affect teams and processes, and develop plans to meet the contingencies that will arise during the change. The most common changes involve technology, process or organizational changes, and consumer habit changes. Externally imposed changes come from new business entrants, or acquisitions and mergers. The "official" objective is to minimize negative behaviors and maximize positive behaviors. Which is a little simplistic. People's behaviors result from their beliefs and attitudes, but also from the quality of leadership and the trust they have in the team and the organization. It is within that context that you manage change. Executives should help individuals operate in an uncertain (we don't know the answers) and ambiguous environment (there are two or three right answers to any question). As such, there are two approaches to managing change.

Where there is some certainty and little ambiguity, one can use the "waterfall" approach to change. Such an approach involves planning for the medium-term future, with the knowledge that the objectives and timeframes will remain relatively constant. It's called a waterfall because once you are in the stream, you are committed to going to the end of the line – it is a linear process. There are many waterfall change methods available, usually following this four-step process: Motivate the change; Plan for the change; Implement; and Monitor and respond.

However, as discussed at some length in this book, business is far from certain, and there are multiple paths to achieving an objective. So long-term plans and goals will probably become redundant well before the planned period. This is why many organizations are adopting agile processes. At its core, it is an incremental process, operating with an overarching goal, accompanied by regular checkpoints. If progress is going well, continue with what's working. If some changes need to be made, pivot the direction, still with the goal in mind. If it's just not working, stop and reevaluate the purpose. Several techniques exist which have adopted these processes – Agile, Scrum, Lean, and Kanban. Agile (with a capital "A") refers to the methodology, while agile (with a small "a") is an adjective. Agile change management methods use the same principles. It is incremental, with a goal in mind, with regular checks on progress. One can continue, pivot or stop. There is another option, where you can choose to delay and carry on when circumstances permit. The Agile philosophy applies to change management as well: People and interactions over processes and tools; working methods over documentation; collaboration over negotiation; and responding to change over following a plan.

COLLABORATION AND DIVERSITY

Command and control or collaborate and lead? That is the question. Command and control is a historic management style based on military principles. It requires a hierarchy, standardization (of people and processes), decision-making at a central command post, and is labor-intensive at best and divisive and demotivating at worst. Leading, guiding, providing meaning, and developing trust, combined with a collaborative culture, is more productive, less stressful, confidence-creating, and motivating. It's a no-brainer.

Collaboration is the process of two or more people working together to complete an undertaking or achieve an objective. Outside the work environment, people collaborate as musicians, sportspeople, and in healthcare, the environment, and academia. The internet has several examples of collaboration: Wikipedia, crowdsourcing, social networks, the free software movement, job gigs, and so on. The purpose of collaboration is to obtain better resources, produce more than the sum of the whole, and achieve more significant objectives. Collaborators share ideas and expertise, develop skills, and have a strong sense of purpose. Most collaboration requires leadership, although in self-managed teams this leadership has a light touch or it devolves to the person most suited to the particular task.

The individual benefit of collaboration is as crucial as the corporate benefit. Executives should establish the team and integrate with their work or get out of the way. Setting up collaborative groups uses similar principles to complex adaptive systems. Provide an overarching purpose, establish a few rules, empower the people in the group, and provide the supporting framework for the team to operate together. Collaboration tools are available to allow people to share ideas and documents, assign tasks to each other and track progress, and communicate with each other either directly or in a forum. Using such software means that teams need not necessarily be located in the same place – in fact, most collaboration today happens from different locations. I collaborate with people in Australia, Europe, and the US without leaving my desk. For face-to-face meetings over the internet, it means coordinating time zones, and sometimes I meet early in the morning or late at night. But that's okay because I manage my own work times.

The skills and attributes required in collaboration teams include a sense of trust, a willingness to encounter and accommodate diverse ideas, open communication, and focus. Collaborative teams should be composed of people with diverse skills and strengths, who are prepared to innovate and be rewarded for it, who delegate tasks to those with the best expertise, and who value difference. Team members should have or develop emotional intelligence, a generic term for someone empathetic, curious, compassionate, resilient, and has systems thinking abilities. Objectives must be clearly defined and agreed, or the team will flounder and lose their way.

With collaboration comes an acceptance of diversity. This is as much acceptance of people with different backgrounds, as acceptance of different ideas, skills, and approaches to work. Diversity is as much about how people identify themselves, as about how others see them. So open communication in a safe space is crucial. Appreciation of diversity means that people elicit viewpoints from quiet or reluctant team members. Each individual should be treated with respect and appreciated for their contribution to the team. Equally, people with diverse backgrounds, skills, and attributes will have blind spots, and the executive should firstly make everyone aware of this circumstance and help people develop the self-awareness to recognize these and accommodate the fact. People who work in diverse teams develop adaptability, a critical attribute for modern business. There is no doubt that people from various backgrounds and with different qualities bring creative ideas and views informed by their experiences and expertise.

RESILIENCE

As Elizabeth Moss Kantor says[8]: "Surprises are the new normal; Resilience is the new skill." On any given workday, an executive will interact with people, make decisions, give a talk or two, receive presentations, handle crises, study new ideas, and have breakfast and lunch meetings. It is not about managing time, so much as managing energy. Resilience is the ability to recover from setbacks, but it is also the ability to maintain strength and enthusiasm for the work to be done and the people to be met.

Steven Snyder says that resilience requires: "… the courage to confront painful realities, the faith that there will be a solution when one isn't immediately evident, and the tenacity to carry on despite a nagging gut feeling that the situation is hopeless."[9] Resilience is not only courage, but it is also the ability to maintain a picture of the goal, to keep things in perspective and maintain purpose. It is also the self-control, reasoning-power, and quietness to do something positive when things are looking bleak. It is the ability to collaborate with others and look after yourself – your health, lifestyle, spirituality, and mental well-being.

Snyder believes that executives develop resilience by adopting a growth mindset – seeking to learn from challenges. They should also develop a support base – both inside the organization and outside. Finally, Snyder suggests that executives get personal – with themselves: Invest time in exercise, self-reflection, and meditation. Adequate and restful sleep is essential, and many functional medicine practitioners (doctors who look at the whole person, not the symptom alone) recommend that fixing circadian rhymes is the first step, before looking into diet, medication, or lifestyle changes. Also, invest time in quietness. There are many more actions executives can take to improve their resilience: Reviewing objectives regularly or reframing goals given the new situation helps maintain perspective and purpose. Other things executives might do is to be solution- not problem-oriented. Giving themselves something to work towards is a way to keep energy levels high. Avoid catastrophizing – imagining the worst that could happen, because it rarely does. Comparing the present with the past or performance with others is not helpful. Much as we might wish it otherwise, today is all we have, so a solutions mindset is essential, while comparisons are not. Comparing performance leads to finding fault – and one set of circumstances and the business environment is fundamentally different from the other.

Ultimately, resilience and all that it encompasses requires having the forms of intelligence, the skills, and attributes of a leader, the ability to deal with complexity, and the wisdom to know when to use each.

NOTES

1 Bruce Nussbaum, *Creative Intelligence: Harnessing the Power to Create, Connect, and Inspire*, HarperCollins, New York, 2013.
2 Claus Møller, *Creative Intelligence*, Claus Møller Consulting, 2005. www.open-windows.se/ow2/doc/Claus_M/Creative_Intelligence-CMC[1].pdf, [Accessed July 2019].
3 Ralph D Stacey, *The Tools and Techniques of Leadership and Management: Meeting the Challenge of Complexity*, Routledge, London, 2012.
4 Bernard McKenna, David Rooney, and Kimberley Boal, Wisdom Principles as a Meta-Theoretical Basis for Evaluating Leadership, *The Leadership Quarterly*, 20, 177-190, 2009.
5 Ben Teehankee, *Arguments against Business Ethics*, Ben Teehankee website. https://sites.google.com/site/benteehankeesite/home/newspaper-columns/arguments-against-business-ethics 2008, [Accessed July 2019].
6 Shane Green, Culture Hacker: Reprogramming Your Employee Experience to Improve Customer Service, *Retention, and Performance*, Wiley, Hoboken, NJ, 2017.
7 Ed Schein, In conversation with Ed Schein, Egonzehnder (Executive Search), July 2019. www.egonzehnder.com/insight/in-conversation-with-ed-schein, [Accessed August 2019].
8 Elizabeth Moss Kantor, Surprises are the New Normal; Resilience is the New Skill, *Harvard Business Review*, 2013. https://hbr.org/2013/07/surprises-are-the-new-normal-r.html, [Accessed June 2019].
9 Steven Snyder, Why Is Resilience So Hard? *Harvard Business Review*, 2013. https://hbr.org/2013/11/why-is-resilience-so-hard, [Accessed July 2019].

CHAPTER FOURTEEN

The evolving organization

EVOLUTION IN A BUSINESS CONTEXT

While natural evolution is a slow, random process beset with false starts, dead ends, and long periods of inactivity, business evolution is a rapid, intentional, active process. However, there are some lessons to be taken from natural evolution and applied to evolving the C-Suite. The first lesson is that we can't wait for evolution to progress naturally in the C-Suite. While we wait, our competition morphs into something we can't catch, or we find we have new competitors who evolved in another industry. Technology is evolving more rapidly every year. Customers evolve as their requirements change and as they scan the internet for new possibilities. Society is changing and regulation evolves to meet risks, challenges, and questionable practices. And products evolve or take evolutionary leaps into new forms. Waiting in business is the path to a dead end.

Not all evolutionary changes are beneficial – in fact, most are neutral and many are harmful. This is where natural selection kicks in. Natural selection is where organisms better adapted to their environment tend to survive and succeed. Those that cope poorly in their environment die off. However, in nature, most natural selection is not about adaptation, but about the preservation of what works well. Although in rapidly changing business circumstances, stasis or maintenance of the status quo means you're going backward, as is the case in the natural world, if every competing species is evolving, those which remain the same will probably fail. Neither is competition straightforward. It can be direct or indirect. In nature, competition can be through competing for, or obstructing access to, a scarce resource – in business, this is the customer. This is called interference competition. Exploitative competition occurs when species compete by consuming the resources that others will use. Where populations increase, exploitative competition rises. Monopolies exhibit both interference and exploitation competition, they also exhibit asymmetric competition, as the largest organization gets access to customers and consumes more resources.

In nature, the size of the gene pool affects evolution, as more and different mutations and combinations are available. In organizations, we've talked about diversity providing new perspectives and ideas. However, as in nature, reproduction is an integral part of the evolutionary cycle. In business, this "reproduction" comes from visionary leadership, feedback loops, and collaboration, all of which we discussed in Chapter 13. The drivers of mutation in natural evolution are radiation or chemicals which change genes, or when DNA fails to copy correctly. By stretching the metaphor, one might liken "radiation" to the always-on, connected, and continually looking customer base. This is the harsh glare in which products are evaluated, and corporate behavior is judged. Again, stretching the metaphor, one might equate the incorrect copying of DNA to accidental inventions or products not used for the purpose they were designed. Accidental inventions include potato crisps which were invented when a customer kept asking for his french fries to be made thinner and crispier. As a joke, the chef fried paper-thin slices of potato and the crisp was born. The microwave oven was invented when an experimenter in radar (microwaves) noticed that a chocolate bar in his pocket melted. Products not used for their original purpose include Bubble Wrap, which was created to be a wallpaper. Brandy was a byproduct of transporting wine when producers boiled off water from wine to cut down on weight and reduce tax levies. So, evolution in business is driven by diversity, vision, collaboration, customer feedback, and happy accidents.

SELF-MANAGED TEAMS

The new and evolving organization is not hierarchical, command- and control-driven or, in many cases, not even located together – Automattic web engineers, the people behind Wordpress.com and other web-based businesses, has over 900 staff in 71 countries and no offices. Instead, they spend their money they would have spent on offices and all the tech that goes with it on supporting their people with technology and travel. Every year they all meet somewhere in the world and the company pays for that. The base unit of the new organization is the self-managed team, operating in a complex-adaptive organization (or self-managing business).

Self-managed teams were first described by Erik Trist and W Bamforth in their 1951 article "Some Social and Psychological Consequences of the Longwall Method of Coal Getting."[1] The title is actually more extended, but then that was how academics presented papers in those days. Subsequently, there were Scandinavian semi-autonomous teams in the 1980s, Semco's self-managed teams in Brazil, and some self-managing organizations like Zappos, Valve, Haier, and Buurtzorg. Several websites report that as many as 80% of US companies have self-managed teams in place. Looking at the original research, what it actually said is that: "...between 70–82% of companies in the United States use the team concept, making teamwork skills one of the most necessary skill sets in the work environment; teamwork tends to promote creativity and problem-solving, high-quality decision-making, and improved communication." There's an issue here and in other research – most organizations had not implemented self-management fully, it was either partial self-management, with some elements retained by the hierarchy (budgets, performance reviews, etc.). Also, the self-managed teams were not in a self-organizing system. The number of organizations that have fully implemented self-managed teams is relatively small compared to traditional hierarchical bureaucracies. Firstly, this is because there are no half-measures, although all organizations mentioned evolved into self-management. Secondly, this is because there is a lot of personal power at stake, and individuals find it hard to adopt the new style. We're looking at organizations that have fully implemented self-managed teams because this is the way to understand the new role of the C-Suite.

Gary Hamel[2] argues that "a hierarchy of managers exacts a hefty tax on any organization" and that "management is the least efficient activity in tour organization." He explains that as an organization grows, if it maintains a ratio of one manager to ten staff, then when it reaches 10,000 people it will have 1,000 managers, and 100 managers to manage them, and 10 managers to manage them. And supposing that each manager earns three times the salary of a first-level employee, then one-third of the wage bill goes to managers. He also argues that decisions take longer, cost more, and are often unworkable. Also, since power increases as you rise up the hierarchy, the higher a decision goes, the less likely it is to be challenged or overturned, leading to the potential for a catastrophic decision. As Hamel says: "Give someone monarch-like authority, and sooner or later there will be a royal screwup." Hamel also believes that if you concentrate decision-making power in a few hands, then personal bias will creep in. That's what this book is about – a C-Suite distant from the workplace, comprised of old white males, will have a bias, particularly when it comes to technology, the thing that is driving and changing business. Finally, Hamel notes that there is the "cost of tyranny," where the hierarchy "systematically disempowers lower-level employees." He observes that as a consumer, someone can spend $20,000 on a new car, but as an employee, they probably don't have the authority to buy a new office chair. Hamel concludes: "Narrow an individual's scope of authority, and you shrink the incentive to dream, imagine, and contribute."

Alternatives to management hierarchies are not only possible, but they are working now, and their companies are, in general, significantly more successful than their bureaucratic competitors. Let me tell you about Morning Star, a food processing company without bosses, titles, or promotions. The company is the world's largest processor of tomatoes, handling about 30% of the USA's tomatoes each year. It makes the products according to their many bulk customer's slightly different recipes. It also produces canned tomatoes, which it ships with its trucking company, and has a business that does the harvesting of the fruit. As it is not a public company, it does not have to report its revenues, but in 2010 it had revenues of over $700 million with 400 employees. If it has continued to grow as it has in the past, its current revenues will be over $1.5 billion. All of this without a single manager. Merely because there's no boss, does not mean that there's no structure, rules, discipline, or accountability – if anything there is more of each, but the employees enforce them ... willingly. The first rule is that the mission is the boss. Each employee develops a personal mission statement and is responsible for accomplishing their mission, and getting the training, resources, and help they need to do so. No-one works alone, of course. They have colleagues dependent on what they produce, colleagues who work with them, and colleagues who they depend on, so every year each employee negotiates a Colleague Letter of Understanding (CLOU – pronounced "clue") with people most affected by their work. A CLOU is

essentially a plan for fulfilling an individual mission. A CLOU can have up
to 30 areas of activity and details the performance goals and metrics for
each area. CLOUs change from year to year to mirror changing priorities,
interests, and competencies – experienced employees take on more complex
tasks and hand more straightforward tasks to newer colleagues. A CLOU
area would look something like: "As a colleague, I agree to provide 20 units
per week, and provide all the paperwork at the end of each day." CLOUs
provide structure and workflows within and between teams. Business units
have CLOU-like agreements with other business units, which are negotiated
annually. As each unit operates a profit and loss account, negotiations can
be cutthroat, haggling over schedules, prices, and volumes. All CLOUs
are governed by the mission statements and the overarching vision of the
company. Since colleagues are responsible for getting the training, resources,
and tools they need to fulfill their mission as planned in the CLOU, there
is no central purchasing department or senior sign-off on expenditures.
Any colleague can issue a purchase order, confirm receipt, and send the
bill to accounting for payment. But, the more the purchase tag, the more
consultation the colleague is expected to do. She is expected to consult with
teammates, financial experts, and negotiation specialists. Colleagues who
buy the same goods, meet with each other regularly to optimize their buying
power. An essential principle at Morning Star is that no-one can order a
colleague to do anything, neither can they veto a decision. For example, the
finance department is concerned with raising capital and giving advice, not
controlling finances and approving purchases.

Self-managed teams are not all brotherhood and fellowship though. James
Barker, in his influential paper: "Tightening the Iron Cage: Concertive
Control in Self-Managing Teams,"[3] notes that control is actually tighter in
such teams compared to bureaucracies. But, he notes that it is agreed by
the team members and imposed by them. He outlines four types of control:
Simple control, which is direct, authoritarian, and personal – best seen in
small companies today; technological control, where control is imposed by
the physical technology – usually an assembly line with workstations; and
bureaucratic control, derived from hierarchies with policies and procedures –
the most common form of commercial control today. The fourth form of

control, Barker says, was posited by Thomkins and Cheney[4] as concertive control where workers collaborate to develop the means of their own control. Here's the issue. The first three forms of control are dominative and imposed from an outside agency, while the fourth is self-control. The difference is crucial. People who exercise self-control in the workplace are happier, motivated, inventive, and importantly, they are more human.

Barker describes an incident where a team member was disciplined by her team for being late to work. When she started crying, they also dissolved in tears and resolved to work the problem out together, explaining that her behavior had affected them all. That's human – tears in the manager's office would possibly be countered with a comment to "pull yourself together!" or worse. One other observation that Barker makes is that in the single organization that he studied over three years, there were three stages in moving to self-management, where, in this case, each stage took about a year. Immediately after the company moved to self-managed teams, there was a period where team members had to establish their roles and purpose and get consensus on how they were going to work together. In this instance, their previous supervisors acted as advisors and facilitators, but not members of the team. The second stage involved the emergence of standards and rules, where the teams decided what the norms of behavior and performance would be. Interestingly, for this company, this stage happened when they took on more new staff than there were existing employees, as their previous self-management efforts had increased the teams from three to six. The "oldies," with a year's experience of self-management, established the "rules" of how to be a functional team. The new team members were left in no doubt that they should fit in or get out. The third stage involves the formalization of the rules. They are put into writing, charts are placed on the wall, and they become more rigid. And Barker observes that this formalization and rigidity are akin to bureaucratic control. However, I come back to my previous observation that it is self-imposed. However, Barker may have a point: Did this company replace its managers with its "oldies?" Was power transferred from managers to long-serving employees? In this case, I think that may be correct, but it may be specific to that organization and those people.

MYTHS ABOUT SELF-MANAGED TEAMS

Not many proponents and authors talk about how to set up these teams. You find different approaches used by various organizations. Some, usually smaller companies, go for the "big bang," while most implement incrementally, which in larger organizations may be the way to go. It seems to me that the setting up of self-managed teams depends on organizational circumstances. However, Nanci Meadows[5] of Dynamic Events and Hubb – an events planning company – probably has the most compelling "how it's done" story. The 35-minute video you'll find on the referenced web address is well worth watching. Nanci says that they had a leadership team of four, who were concerned about the toxic environment, their own workload, and the performance of the company. They believed that there had to be a better way of doing things and through research and some introspection, decided that self-managed teams were a possible answer. They were excited about the concept and talked about it all the time. As Meadows says: "This freaked our people out." Even though their staff were unhappy in their work, they preferred that to the unfamiliar. So the leadership team realized their first mistake – they weren't communicating or including their people on the journey. They organized a one-day workshop with all their people where they explored the myths about self-management.

The first myth is that there's no structure. No management, leadership, or boss, to tell people what to do. But, there is. Leadership occurs naturally, falling to the person in the team with the appropriate expertise, responsibility, and experience, and leadership changes with the task to be undertaken. In teams, there's seldom a dispute over who leads, because the team knows themselves and each other. The second myth is that everyone is equal. But people's abilities, experience, and expertise are not equal, so people give and take according to what they can contribute, and according to what needs to be done.

The third myth is that self-managed teams are a way of empowering people. It is not. Doug Kirkpatrick, one of the original people at Morning Star and now a self-management consultant and speaker, puts empowerment in its place like this: "Empowerment is where one person with power is lending some of their power to a subordinate with less power. And what is loaned, can be repossessed. Self-management is beyond empowerment ... it is power itself."[6]

The fourth myth is that decisions are made by consensus. In self-managed teams, decisions are made by the person most able to make the decision. This does not mean that everyone makes decisions about everything. The most appropriate person to make a decision about work is the person who is doing the work. It's much like the first myth – if leadership occurs naturally, then decisions also occur naturally.

Meadows goes on to identify some of the critical differences between traditional hierarchies and self-managed companies, which I've added to, as shown in Table 14.1:

Table 14.1 Differences between traditional organizations and self-managed teams

	Traditional organization	Self-managed teams
The boss	People are appointed as bosses, by their bosses.	The mission is the boss. There is no organization chart showing who works for whom.
Titles	Titles indicate position and authority.	Titles indicate a role; used for external purposes only; people choose their title.
Power	Power is vested in the hierarchy.	Power is vested in the people who do the work, they have the authority to get it done.
Information	Information is power, and available to managers.	Information drives self-managed teams. Their effectiveness comes from acting on information.
Management	Employees report to managers; subordinate and supervisor.	People manage commitments not people.
Owning the problem	Problems are escalated "upward," often with strict protocols.	People own the challenge; call on others to help out; trained in radical candor.
Objectives	Management determines the goals, and how they are to be reached.	Leaders determine the goals, teams decide how to reach them.
Hierarchy	In any hierarchy, an "us" versus "them" mentality arises.	We're all "us," with specific skills and contributions.

COMPLEX-ADAPTIVE ORGANIZATIONS

The business world is both complex and complicated. "Complicated" involves many moving parts, but the result for any complicated system is the same each time. "Complex" includes many moving parts which change in response to inputs and conditions. The result is usually different every time. We've spent much of the book describing how factors which affect the business environment are continuously changing, and that the rate of change is increasing. It should be no surprise then, that I believe that we need to be able to respond to a complex situation appropriately, flexibly, and in time to have an effect. I've also spent a good part of the book explaining that a hierarchy cannot sense and respond to changing conditions in the time available, or in the appropriate manner needed to accommodate the change, or indeed, with the necessary flexibility to change and keep changing. For that you need a complex-adaptive organization. The term "complex-adaptive" doesn't mean the organization is complex, instead, that it is adaptive to complex circumstances. In fact, a complex-adaptive organization is quite simple – so simple that most people struggle to understand the simplicity.

The elements of a complex-adaptive organization are an overarching vision – what Frederic Laloux calls an "evolutionary purpose." We need a few fractal axioms (a principle that is self-evidently true) – Nanci Meadows calls these "primary tenets." And we need agents with autonomy – we all call them self-managed teams. Finally, we need an environment in which all this can happen. That's it. Too simple? Let's unpack these four elements starting with the concept of fractals.

I won't go into the mathematical definition of fractals. Instead, I will borrow from two fractal concepts to move us to complex-adaptive organizations. First, fractals are small and simple components. Second, they are recursive – simply put, when multiplied by themselves, they create a larger structure. In nature, a tree, river delta, or a snowflake is a building up of small dendritic structures to form the whole. Nautilus shells, various aloes, and plants exhibit growth spirals, which are a fractal form. In organizations, much of bureaucracy is fractal – small rules having significant effects on the effectiveness, either positive or negative. In complex-adaptive organizations, real care needs to be given to the development of fractal axioms – luckily many organizations have gone before us, and we can borrow from them, for example: "The mission is the boss," is a small statement which will have significant consequences if the agents in the organization obey the fractal axiom. Similarly, the Morning Star tenet of: "honor commitments," led to fractal effects in the organization.

Let's get back to the purpose or vision element of a complex-adaptive organization. I prefer Laloux's term evolutionary purpose since that makes it adaptive purpose – and constant adaptation is everything. Except in very few organizations, the purpose of the company is set by the leadership team. And rightly so, I think, since their new role in the C-Suite is the management of meaning and attention: "What's happening out there (and in here), what does it mean for us, and how can we get everyone to attend to it?" Meadows talks about leadership, providing the "what" and self-managed teams providing the "how." It's one of their company's fractal axioms. So it's leadership's job to understand "why we exist" and "what we need to do to survive and thrive." In several companies, the leaders realized that moving to self-managed teams was a matter of survival. In currently self-organizing companies, it's instructive to see what they define as their purpose. Buurtzorg, the home-nursing organization, says that it aims for "self-managing clients." There's a fractal purpose if ever. Add that to their tagline: "Humanity over bureaucracy," and merely those two fractals have spawned a revolutionary and very successful operation. The Buurtzorg CEO's job is to "think about things" and be the face of the organization. Nanci Meadows' company is an event company that wants to create "moments of impact." An evolutionary purpose needs to evolve in response to conditions.

I won't go into "agents with autonomy" – that's self-managed teams – but it is useful to consider the "environment in which all this can happen." We're talking about culture and, for want of a better word, infrastructure. Initially, a complex-adaptive organization needs a culture of permission. The habits of boss-subordinate, them and us, and "they have the power and it's not my problem – it's management's," and "I just do my job and they tell me what it is" can be stultifying to all employees, management, and staff alike.

We have to operate in the current paradigm. The word "paradigm" has been polluted over time, and now it seems to mean: "the way things are done." The real meaning is sort of related in that it means: "a framework containing the basic assumptions, ways of thinking, and methodology that are commonly accepted by a group of people." Three elements in the formal definition warrant attention: A paradigm is a framework, it is a set of assumptions, and it is a way of thinking. In the current paradigm, the framework is the hierarchy; it assumes that hierarchies are the only way of running a business and thinks that top-down decisions are the only way to get things done. So, within the current organizational paradigm, someone high up needs to make a decision to permit others to think. Even in start-ups, as happened in Morning Star, the CEO had to allow others to think. In a workshop with his senior managers, before the company had even produced their first tomato product, Chris Rufer said something like:

> What if there were no bosses, and the mission is the boss. And what if people should not use force or coercion against other people. And what if people honored the commitments they made. Could we run our company with those three rules?

But by calling the workshop and asking, "what if …," Rufer was giving permission to his team to think. It's more difficult in currently running companies, because not only do you have to give permission to think, but you also have to help people unthink. In an established organization, giving people permission to unthink is more complicated. You have to give people a compelling reason for the self-organizing route the company must take, you have to deal with management and executives who believe they will lose power, prestige, and pay. This is not easy to do.

Alan Weiss, an organizational consultant with a PhD in psychology, once said: "Managers hang onto their power and privilege like monkeys onto a branch. You have to prise them off or murder them. Our managers won't be prised, we are going to have to kill them."[7] I wouldn't go that far, but privilege and power are potent motivators for resistance to change. Paul Strebel, author of "The Change Pact,"[8] classified people in organizations into change agents, resistors, bystanders, and traditionalists. You deal with each type differently: Change agents are for the change, and you "satisfy" them – provide all the resources they need, be available to listen and discuss, and generally ease their way through the organization. Resistors are against the change, fitting into Alan Weiss's category of managers holding onto their power – you dissatisfy them, doing the opposite of what you do with change agents. Bystanders are disengaged, and you give them as much information as possible, while traditionalists hang onto the old way of doing things. Their chief motivator is security, so you offer security only in the new environment. It is difficult, but I've seen satisfy/ dissatisfy strategy work remarkably well. Change agents drive enthusiasm and often convert resistors. Alternatively, resistors stripped of their power move on.

For non-managers, you need to provide the same reasons and information you would to managers, dispel myths about self-organization, and organize open discussions about the change to come. Remember that in self-organizing environments, the leaders provide the "what" and the teams provide the "how." It is a good thing to do early in the program, because it engages people, establishes some ground rules, and readies them for self-management.

That deals with the "permission" part of the cultural change. Dynamic Events, a self-managed company, says on their website: "Our culture is intentional." This is critical. The few fractal axioms should be structured so they guide how work is done but should also be the building blocks of the culture of the organization.

The infrastructure of a complex-adaptive organization is set up to allow the free flow of information and access to resources and should allow decisions to be taken by team members. Usually, such organizations have a central portal where information is available, not only on how the company and business units are performing but also where methods, solutions, and tips and tricks are open to all teams. This portal should also allow questions and answers and general discussions on directions and goals to be posted. People gain stature and power through their contribution to others and the organization, and populating these portals is a way of contributing. I have heard of a few organizations that have their own Wiki, where people update the current knowledge on a particular subject or way of doing things. Such a Wiki would be invaluable for onboarding new staff and keeping the company knowledge current. Some self-managed organizations have workflow and collaboration systems. Many self-managing organizations have shared services units, like finance and accounts, and human resources (I hate that term – perhaps it should be called "the people performance team"), which assist with take-on of new staff, payroll, training, and facilitating the people processes in the organization. There is a danger here of setting up fiefdoms, but remember, the mission is the boss. So, within the organization's mission these units should craft their purpose in the service of the teams. They should operate as self-managed teams with profit and loss statements, letters of understanding with other groups and individuals, and should be a *service* to colleagues.

Finally, the infrastructure should provide feedback loops that allow the organization to sense and respond. Such feedback can comprise the leadership team, one of whose primary roles is the sensing of trends, threats, and developments in the organization's ecosystem. Other feedback can come from technology. IoT (the Internet of Things) is a sensory network of devices that provide information on production and on customers. (A mobile device can be networked as an IoT device.) Similarly, AI (artificial intelligence) is a sense and respond technology, especially if it is tied to IoT. AI is relatively cheap and straightforward to set up, and its value to a complex-adaptive organization is that it removes drudgework from teams.

Complex-adaptive organizations rely on four simple concepts, but their response is not linear or pre-programmed. They adapt to complex environments, which is the environment of most businesses today.

NOTES

1   Erik Trist and W Bamforth, Some Social and Psychological Consequences of the Long Wall Method of Coal-Getting, *Human Relations*, 4, 3-38, 1951.

2   Gary Hamel, First, Let's Fire All the Managers, *Harvard Business Review*, December 2011.

3   James Barker, Tightening the Iron Cage: Concertive Control in Self-Managing Teams, *Administrative Science Quarterly*, 38(3), 408-437, 1993.

4   Phillip Tompkins and George Cheney, Communication and Unobtrusive Control in Contemporary Organizations. In Robert D. McPhee and Phillip K. Tompkins (eds.), *Organizational Communication: Traditional Themes and New Directions*: 179-210. Newbury Park, CA: Sage, 1985.

5   Rosie Powers, *Self-Managed Teams: Creating Innovation from Autonomy*, TINYpulse, 2019. www.tinypulse.com/blog/self-managed-teams-creating-innovation-from-autonomy, [Accessed August 2019].

6   Doug Kirkpatrick, *Beyond Empowerment – Are We Ready for the Self-Managed Organization?*, TEDxChico, 2013. www.youtube.com/watch?v=Ej4n3w4kMa4, [Accessed August 2019].

7   Alan Weiss, *Our Emperors Have No Clothes: Incredibly Stupid Things Corporate Executives Have Done While Reengineering, Restructuring, Downsizing, TQM'ing, Team-Building, and Empowering … In Order to Cover their Ifs, ands, or "Buts"*, Career Press Inc., Newburyport, MA, 1995.

8   Paul Strebel, *The Change Pact: Building Commitment to Ongoing Change*, Pitman Publishing, London, 1998.

CHAPTER FIFTEEN

Evolving the C-Suite

THE CHANGE IS INTERNAL

"The only real revolution is in the enlightenment of the mind and the improvement of character, the only real emancipation is individual, and the only real revolutionists are philosophers and saints." These are the words of Will and Ariel Durant, who spent four decades studying, compiling, and writing the history of Western civilization, published in 11 books. You don't have to read them all, thank goodness, since they also produced a book called "The lessons of history"[1] from which the above quote comes. Even their short book is a dense read, but luckily Zat Rana wrote an article called, "It's Not What You Know, It's How You Think,"[2] taking their most important lesson from their book. The Durants considered that notwithstanding all that has and continues to change in our environment, the battle is internal. People don't change if their minds don't change.

Rana goes on to observe that our minds get stuck in habit loops as a matter of survival and as a matter of making our way through life without having to make decisions about mundane issues. However, habit loops can hold us back when faced with new challenges, and the way to get clear of them, if we are even aware of them, is to challenge our thinking by seeking out new environments, reading, and considering hypothetical thought games.

I suspect that most executives will not embark on a self-managing team approach or on an adaptive organization route because as Rick Wartzman[3] says: "The less hierarchy at a company, the more that certain people will be forced to give up their perks and privileges … we're asking the princes to lay down their crowns." And that's it. Self-management and adaptive organizations appear to remove power, prestige, and pay from the people who have the power to implement them. I say "appear" because in all my reading and experience of self-management it seems that these roadblocks to change are surmountable and the resultant performance of the organization proves that it was the right thing to do. So, two things: If you find yourself resistant to change, which will improve company performance, perhaps you could think about your ethical standpoint; and if you find yourself thinking that this can never work, perhaps your habit loops are driving you. Either way, the battle is internal and it's yours.

In Chapter 14, I covered how to introduce self-managed teams and complex-adaptive organizations by applying change management techniques, supplying reasons and information, and creating an environment in which to succeed. However, this is about executives in the C-Suite who need to challenge and change themselves. Here, we can take direction from the many resources available on overcoming limiting beliefs. A limiting belief is a belief that constrains us in some way. Just by believing them, we do not think, do or say the things that they inhibit. My idea of identifying a limiting belief is to find something that challenges me. Often the challenge hides a limiting belief. In Chapter 11, I touched on three possible limiting beliefs of executives. One is that you can do everything necessary. This is not possible and moving to a self-managing team structure challenges that belief directly. A second is that you can find a solution to everything. Again, self-managed teams work on the answer to problems and challenges that executives identify. Finally, many executives use their past experience to address new issues. We've covered the generation issues, and while most executives are Baby Boomers and early Generation X, their self-managed teams are all from generations who bring fresh perspectives to problems.

Dealing with limiting beliefs follows a pattern: Firstly, identify areas that challenge you. Secondly, identify the beliefs that you have about the challenge. Let's take the setting up of self-managed teams as a challenge, which it certainly is. I've covered the myths around self-managed teams. No-one is in control. There's no structure, everyone is equal, and decisions are made by consensus and are slow. These are myths and have not been proven to be true. The next step after identifying a limiting belief is to test whether you absolutely know it to be true. Are there reliable experts or sources of information which prove the truth or falsehood of the belief? If it's not true, then … it's not true. Devise a belief that is the opposite of the limiting belief, for instance, as we've seen, James Barker showed that there was more control with self-managed teams. We've also seen that with the right overarching purpose and fractal axioms, structure imposes itself – it self-organizes. Finally, decisions have been proven to be faster and more sound than in a hierarchical organization. So new truths would be: "Control will be improved, structure emerges naturally, and decisions happen quickly, in self-managed teams."

WHAT DOES THE EVOLVED C-SUITE DO?

In Chapter 13, we went through the attributes required to be an executive in the C-Suite. He or she must have spatial, intrapersonal, and interpersonal intelligence, as well as the norm of logical and linguistic intelligence. Executives must be able to handle complexity. Additionally, they must be ethical and wise. They need resilience, a collaborative mindset, and must value diversity. Finally, digital fluency is an essential skill they need to develop. Many executives already have these attributes, but there are areas that they may need to work on.

Much of part two of this book deals with what an evolved C-Suite will do. That's why this section is short – the building blocks are already defined. It's a small challenge to consolidate the information into a coherent plan.

Assuming the C-Suite is committed to self-managed teams and building a complex-adaptive organization, they have two types of role to play – during the initiation stage and in the ongoing phase. During the initiation of self-organization, executives need to explore self-management concepts and develop their mental model of how it could work in their organization. They need to present their case for change to each other and to the people in the organization. They also should craft the overarching purpose, which will drive all personal missions in their teams. Research has shown that companies with a purpose outperform those with only a profit motive: Gartenberg and Serafeim[4] found that: "… companies with high levels of purpose outperform the market by 5%–7% per year, on par with companies with best-in-class governance and innovative capabilities. They also grow faster and have higher profitability." They also found that there is only a link between purpose and profitability if senior executives communicate that purpose and the organization adopts that purpose as their own. Part of the overarching purpose is what John Hagel[5] calls a zoom-in/zoom-out strategy, which zooms out on substantial long-term opportunities they see emerging on a ten-year horizon. Then it zooms in on two or three initiatives that can be pursued in the next year to accelerate progress towards the long-term opportunity or to challenge and amplify opportunities to learn by doing. He says: "The goal is to inspire everyone with a very significant opportunity to create much more impact, but also focus on near-term action that can start to demonstrate impact."

Driving the change requires leadership and guidance, as well as interpersonal skills. Remember that the leadership team decides on the "what," while the teams work on the "how." The leadership team doesn't and can't do everything, and neither should they because that's why self-managed teams are being set up. Set the direction, let the teams engage with it, having leaders guiding them all the way. Look to the internal infrastructure to ensure that the tools, information, and the culture supports the teams. Keep in mind that the business environment is moving along swiftly, so the leadership team needs to be looking outward as well.

The "routine" phase, once the self-managed teams are set up, involves the leadership team as the front of the organization, the "requirements" engine, and the guidance team where needed. The front of the organization consists of representing the company to the outside world: Customers, suppliers, shareholders, analysts, government, and regulatory bodies.

The second and third roles of the C-Suite in a self-organizing organization relate to the tenet "Leaders decide on the what, and teams decide the how." This doesn't mean that teams cannot work on the "what," but the primary role of leaders is outward-looking, while teams are largely inward-looking. The two functions of leaders in establishing what needs to be done speak to Warren Bennis's notion that leaders manage meaning and attention.

In managing meaning, C-Suite scan the environment for developments, challenges, and changes which mean something to the organization.

For instance, in an event management company, robotics may not have meaning to them but will have meaning to a manufacturing business. Similarly, developments in online web-based meetings and webinars will have meaning to the events company, but perhaps not to the manufacturing company. Context is important and is usually derived from both the vision and the mission of the organization. A note on vision and mission – the vision of the organization defines what they aspire to, and the mission is why they exist. For instance, the events company might have a vision of organizing every major corporate gathering in the communications industry, while their mission might be the organization of game-changing events in the communications industry. They don't need to be mutually exclusive, but the vision targets *every* major event, and the mission says they organize *game-changing* events. Both inform the scanning context, and both contextualize the meaning for the organization.

The management of attention is the third role of the C-Suite. To do so, they take events and challenges which have meaning for the organization and develop mental models of how these fit with organizational objectives. For example, in the events management company, the C-Suite believes that online webinars mean that they can offer attendance at a conference even if the delegate cannot be at the conference. They also think that speakers can give presentations from a distance, or they might be able to record their presentation, which, although not ideal, may provide an essential talk at the conference. Finally, the latest development in webinars allows participation, voting, and theme development, which may continue long after the conference is over. The mental model would include an explanation of the webinar functionality and would be followed by a "what if" set of statements:

- What if people who can't attend a conference could sign in and watch from wherever they are?
- What if we provided a portal where all attendees could update a profile of their interests and challenges?
- What if we have a 'theme consolidator,' which tells people that say, fifteen people are battling with interconnectivity issues in their business ecosystem?
- What if all this would take conference networking to another level?

Such statements, with a description of the tech which would make this possible, grab the teams' attention and they set them up for what the C-Suite thinks will take the company to the next level. There's no need to define the goal in great detail; in fact, it is undesirable, as you want to cultivate innovation and free-thinking in the teams.

I was having a conversation last night with an HR executive of a large pharmaceutical company, and she suggested that if leaders decide the "what," and teams work on the "how," then nothing will stop teams doing their own thing. And she asked how leaders made teams do the "what." Let me be clear. Leaders lead. They don't make anyone do anything.

Which brings us to role number four for the C-Suite – looking after the environment in the organization. I've said that the organizational environment includes culture and infrastructure.

Leading the culture requires that the C-Suite ensures that teams have autonomy (freedom to act on their mission) and independence (within the fractal axioms and the overarching mission). This is not as easy as it sounds since executives must allow mistakes. As Nanci Meadows of Dynamic Events says: "Mistakes are how we learn, and rarely are these mistakes catastrophic." In fact, with the checks and balances in place in collaborating teams and people, and given the mission of each individual, mistakes are significantly rarer than in management hierarchies. A sidetrack here: I know of a bank that spent over $1 billion on a software package that never delivered. The problem now is that the bank continues hammering the software solution into place, and racking up more costs, not to mention running inefficiently. Egos are involved – the executives cannot admit that the original decision was a mistake, neither can they take another tack, because to do so would get them fired. There, I've had my rant. Autonomy and independence, with the mistakes that it might bring, build confidence and a learning mindset.

Leading the culture also requires that the C-Suite continually attend to the fractal axioms. Not to change them, but to see that they are being adhered to. Self-management is not a free for all. Where executives find the rules being bent or flouted is a timely opportunity to have the discussion on the rules and whether they need to be changed – many hierarchies operate on out-of-date rules. If the fractal axiom is still sound, the discussion can move onto how they are being bent or broken, and how (remember that's the teams' job) they can be applied. In Chapter 14 I noted that James Barker found that control strengthened in a self-organizing system and, importantly, this control is not imposed from "above" but agreed to and followed by teams because they want to. Rules set boundaries, but the limits are best set when decided upon by the people who are to work within them.

Communication, collaboration, and alignment are also essential parts of leading the culture. Executives should communicate often, collaborate with each other and with the teams, and be aligned both with the vision and mission and with each other. Similarly, they should give thought to easing communication, collaboration, and alignment in the team domain, and here we come to the other part of managing the organizational environment – infrastructure. The word infrastructure derives from the Latin "infra-" and "-structure." "Infra-" means below or beneath, and "-structure" derives from "structus" meaning arrangement or order. So my use of the word infrastructure in this context is that it is the supporting arrangement and order below the operations of the organization.

So, my meaning of infrastructure means that it is more than offices, equipment, and technology. It is these things, of course, but it is also the feedback loops, the skills, and the information, all of which are needed to ensure that self-managed teams operate effectively. If it seems a lot, consider the costs of the hierarchy. Managers take about 30% of the salary bill in a hierarchy – not including the office space – and, frankly, damage the organization with the slow and often bad decisions they make. This doesn't include the opportunity cost of no decisions being made by team members, or that 87% of people are not engaged at work and are therefore merely "doing their job" and no more – no innovation, passion, or … engagement with work.

Office infrastructure has changed and continues to evolve. It should especially do so with self-managed teams. In Chapter 6 I said: "… so fixed office space is less important to them as collaborative areas, project rooms, discussion areas, and hot-desking." Also, it has been shown that open-plan offices reduce productivity. Teams work better as teams. So hubs should be made available to house the team and no-one else.

Equipment is less of an issue for the C-Suite, since in self-managed teams people are responsible for getting the training, resources, and tools they need to fulfill their mission. If they have a P&L (profit and loss) statement, they know if the team can afford the equipment. The trick for the leadership team is to stay out of the way. To do otherwise would undermine team autonomy.

A central element of self-managed team infrastructure is feedback. In all self-managed organizations, information is available to all, rather than the leadership team alone. As discussed in Chapter 1, information is a form of power, and power is hard for traditional executives to give up. However, the only way self-management can work is if teams have access to all the information – both their team's and other teams'. Feedback is essential to allow teams to sense and respond. They need to manage their performance, finances, and commitments. They also manage their own reviews of how they and individuals in the team are doing and decide the metrics for their performance to meet their mission. An executive's role in this is to ensure that information is available and flows freely.

Another component of the organization's "infrastructure" is the capabilities and skills of the people in teams, while teams are responsible for building their skills so they can do their job. However, experience with self-managed teams has shown that there are generic skills needed which would not usually appear on the menu for employees in hierarchies. Individuals in self-managed teams need to develop financial, negotiation, and conflict management skills. Also, since they are taking on the roles of managers, they should look to project planning and management as a skill.

ADDRESSING CHALLENGES TO THE C-SUITE

Probably the most significant challenge to the C-Suite is the C-Suite executives. They have age, prestige, power, and ego against them. Having risen through the ranks and "arrived," they may be reluctant to give up the prestige and power, not to mention the remuneration.

However, none of these are at risk if they create a complex-adaptive organization and self-managed teams. The new role of C-Suite executives will give them power to decide on the strategic direction, and lead the discussion on what the organization needs to do to execute the strategy. However, if an executive equates power to control, they will be resistant until they understand that self-managed teams achieve more control than they could. If, on the other hand, they equate power with dominance, then the problem is intractable. I believe that the majority of executives are not into domination, and if they hold the interests of their organization and their people to heart, sound executives will work through their own issues.

The new role of the C-Suite executives provides, to my mind, greater prestige than in a hierarchy. They are the face of the organization, representing it to the market, customers, shareholders, and other stakeholders. Not only that, but their prestige is enhanced because of the work they do – they engage with trends and developments, develop mental models, and gain the attention of not only their staff but their ecosystem and industry as well. There is, I believe, significant prestige in leading a self-organizing company – the executive has risen above the norm and has dared to do things differently. Finally, the better performance of the company brings its own prestige.

Probably the biggest challenge outside the C-Suite involves the material they have to work with – people. Both executives and the C-Suite are products of the education system and the society in which we live. The education system was dealt with in Chapter 2 and it presents business with factory-ready graduates. If the system has been successful, people presenting themselves for work are numerate and literate, but they are also compliant and convergent thinkers. They may not be creative, innovative, independent, autonomous, and team players – all the things we are looking for in a self-organizing environment. Their alternate intelligences have not been nurtured – their spatial, intrapersonal, and interpersonal intelligence has not been developed at school. Luckily, modern technology and creative pedagogy allow us to do something about that. Education is freely available, or inexpensive on the internet. Online guides and mentors can help guide people. Executives should help staff with divergent thinking. To recap: Divergent thinking is creative and generates options, while convergent thinking forms judgments and produces solutions. Both are needed, of course, but the dominance of convergent over divergent thinking has been inculcated into people since school-going age. This takes some undoing. One of the things an executive might do is tap into the skills of the teams, many of whom will definitely be more skilled than the executive. Another tactic is to relish the chance of teaching others. Another tactic would be to establish centers of excellence, staffed by experienced and able people, with the role of teaching others and also of improving the environment – the culture and infrastructure (as defined in the section before this). Another skill which might prove useful is the methods in Agile work. These include Lean, Kanban, Scums, and MVP (Minimum Viable Products).

One challenge that some self-managing organizations have faced is the lack of titles. As Nanci Meadows of Dynamic Events said: "Titles are for interfacing with the external environment – some people move on and to help their career path, they find it useful to have a title which describes their role. Our people choose their own titles."

There are several challenges for the C-Suite to face in self-organizing companies, and a significant one is dealing with the ecosystem into which the business falls. This is part of the outward-facing role of executives and should be nothing more than explaining to suppliers, customers, partners, and other stakeholders how to deal with your organization. Some external people will want to talk to the "boss," and where there are no bosses, some explanation might be necessary.

The evolved C-Suite executives will be challenged in their new roles, and they will emerge over time. This means that executives will be busy – first, actualizing the new way of working, then, assuming their "routine" C-Suite roles as leaders, facilitators, guides, and above all, thinkers about the big issues.

NOTES

1 Will Durant and Ariel Durant, *The Lessons of History*, Simon & Schuster, New York, 2010.

2 Zat Rana, It's Not What You Know, It's How You Think, *Medium*. https://medium.com/s/story/the-trick-to-thinking-clearer-and-better-4a61c54114fa, 2018, [Accessed August 2019].

3 Rick Wartzman, If Self-Management Is Such a Great Idea, Why Aren't More Companies Doing It? *Forbes*, 2012. www.forbes.com/sites/drucker/2012/09/25/self-management-a-great-idea/#1cfb974a11de, [Accessed August 2019].

4 Claudine Gartenberg and George Serafeim, 181 Top CEOs Have Realized Companies Need a Purpose beyond Profit, *Harvard Business Review*, August 2019.

5 John Hagel, "Institutional Innovation – I Have a Dream", *Edge Perspectives*, January 2019. https://edgeperspectives.typepad.com/edge_perspectives/2019/01/institutional-innovation-i-have-a-dream.html, [Accessed July 2019].

CHAPTER SIXTEEN

The way forward – the transition of the C-Suite

The late Charles Reich, a visiting professor at Yale Law School, in his 1995 book: "Opposing the system,"[1] talks about how individuals have no power, being beholden to the organizations who pay their salaries, and governments have diminished power as everything they do is in the open, and political incumbents have a four- to five-year tenure. Businesses, with their profit motive, cannot serve human needs, nor does the focus on growth consider the costs like urban decay, family breakup, environmental degradation or, indeed, the future – for many executives it's me, me, me, and now, now, now. Reich considered that the Bill of Rights is regularly violated in the workplace. The business system was responsible for the corporate raiding of America and the entrenchment of a managerial elite whose only motive is profit for the few, he said, and believed that "we need a new consciousness." There is no doubt that Reich's book is polemic in nature, but many of the points he makes ring true for all that. Charles Handy believed that corporations were not democratic in any way.

Could we label traditional hierarchical corporations as inefficient, ineffective, and immoral as well? I think this is a little harsh, perhaps, but there is a definite need to change the way we organize and run our businesses. To understand where we are in the new way of organizing and running companies, we should look at the theory of "Diffusion of Innovations," a book published by Everett Rogers in 1962. The book is in its fifth edition and became the second-most cited book in the social sciences. The book deals with how innovations spread and are adopted, and social scientists took the concepts to explain how people assume new ideas.

ADOPTING NEW IDEAS

Rogers presented a "diffusion of innovations" curve,[2] which explains how innovations and ideas are adopted by people. I've modified his seminal curve as shown in Figure 16.1:

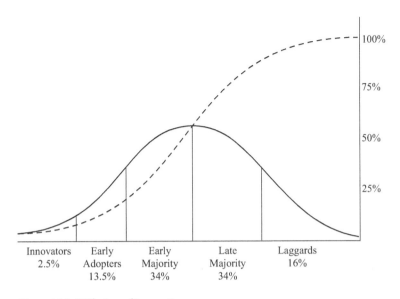

Figure 16.1 Diffusion of innovation curve

Innovators invent or initiate the idea or concept, while early adopters are visionaries, who know something useful when they see it and don't need reference sites to try it out. They are change agents who want to get radical performance improvements and get ahead of the competition. The early majority are pragmatic, have seen the idea in action, and have some solid case studies to base their adoption of the concept upon. They want to minimize disruption and are looking for enhanced improvements in performance. The late majority sees others being successful, and need to catch up with them, and the laggards are, well … laggards.

If, as some researchers say, self-managed teams are adopted by 70–82% of companies in the USA, then we should be well into the late majority stage, which is patently not true. I would suggest that we are in the early adopter phase, heading into the early majority. Geoffrey Moore places a "chasm"[3] between the early adopters and the early majority. He reasons that many ideas and products get some initial support, but lose out before the early majority stage. VHS crossed the chasm, Beta did not even though it was a theoretically better product. Microsoft Word crossed, but Wordperfect and Wordstar did not, despite being better applications. The signs that an idea is approaching the chasm are a convergence of standards and terms, an increasing body of knowledge, and individual use cases, which is where I believe self-managed teams are today. There is general acceptance of what a self-managed team is, and there is a growing body of knowledge about how to set them up and run them. Finally, there are now several solid examples of organizations that have implemented them and been successful. I believe that self-management will cross the chasm – as a practice, it's cheaper, faster, more agile, and more innovative. The factor that will stop this crossing is the C-Suites of traditional hierarchies. Their self-interest, egos, power, and investment in the status quo are a formidable force. Also, progressive companies sometimes revert back to traditional methods because of a leadership change – so we're back to the C-Suite again. However, the C-Suite does not operate in a vacuum. Even within the C-Suite, some executives have the foresight and courage to change before change is imposed upon them. Shareholders have the most sway in forcing the change, because it is in *their* self-interest to increase revenues and decrease costs, and self-management has been shown to do that. Inside the organization, some people have influence and far-sightedness and can both lobby and set up their own self-managed teams, admittedly within the constraints imposed on them by the hierarchy – a resistance movement if you like. Once a self-managing team is producing better results than hierarchical teams and units, there are potential allies to be found in shareholders – better, cheaper, and faster production is a strong incentive for shareholders to take to the executive team. The business ecosystem and partners can also do the same, approaching principal shareholders to see if they can "help" bring their companies up to the same speed as the ecosystem.

TECHNIQUES FOR CHANGE

Techniques needed to effect this change will include oration and debate, research and intuition, bypassing and including, starving and feeding, satisfying and dissatisfying, and, indeed, any method which can get results. Most of all, a learning mindset and ecosystems thinking is required.

The media, researchers, advocates, and books deliver the sermon. What is needed is a debate, both within organizations and in the public space. One place I find the most lucid discussion about the new work and organization is Corporate Rebels (www.corporate-rebels.com), who are two people who left their corporate jobs and now tour the world visiting inspiring organizations. While on their travels, they share everything they learn, both the positive and negative aspects of corporate change. Much of the material about self-organizing systems appears to state that it is further along the adoption path than I think it is. That corporates need to change is without question in my mind – I think it's a matter of survival. Therefore, advocates of corporate survival and people who are alarmed by corporate excesses should continue to deliver the message and lead the debates.

Executives should be able to use both research and intuition to arrive at a decision. It is no different in this case. The research is there for those who want to find it. There's a lot of hype as well, but that is only exponents enthusiastically doing their thing. It is time for executives to use a little intuition, examine how they feel about their existing environment, and question whether there is a better way.

"Bypassing and including" is a tactic that can break logjams. I already talked about how employees can bypass corporate bureaucracy, control, and power games by setting up their own self-managed teams within the organization, and, once successful, approach shareholders with evidence of what is possible. Alternatively, they might find a progressive executive and include him or her in their plans. Another aspect of bypassing traditional hierarchies lies in what is called the "Edge Organizations." These units are set up at the edge of organizations. John Hagel[4] believes that organizations have immune systems and antibodies that act to destroy any threat to the status quo, which is why you build significant change at the edge. Anthony Alston[5] contends that Edge Organizations should follow an autonomous organizational form where power is moved away from the center to those involved in execution. An Edge Organization is encouraged to practice divergent thinking, generating options and testing possibilities and accepted norms, far away from the reductionist thinking of the central organization with its plans, rules, and control structures. Hagel also believes that Edge Organizations should be constrained in the resources and funding they have available to them to promote innovation to move beyond the constraints. If funded and supported fully, the Edge Organization may simply replicate the central organization. Here's where the "starving and feeding" aspect comes in. The primary organization starves the Edge Organization of resources and funding, but "feeds" them with autonomy and freedom to act.

Finally, as Paul Strebel[6] proposed, one can "satisfy" the change agents and "dissatisfy" the resistors. In Strebel's change model, he suggests that about 90% of people in organizations are passive – and the research shows that 87% are disengaged. Typically only 10% of people are active, either for or against the change. Those people who are actively for the change are called change agents, and those actively against are resistors. When inside the organization, unlike in Edge Organizations, one provides change agents with the resources and funding they need to get the change made. Similarly, one dissatisfies resistors by starving them of resources and funds. It's using power for good. I suppose because I have seen power used oppositely – where the noisiest get the resources – I worry about the abuse or misuse of power.

For now, executives wield power and exercise control, often to their own ends, and take their authority from the hierarchical system. As Frederic Laloux[7] says:

> Leaders in large organizations seem all-powerful, and, like all of us, they want to look like their life is in control like they are winners in the game of success. But anyone who has had a chance to have intimate conversations with organizational leaders knows that behind the façade, almost all of them are tired – tired of the rat race and the pressure, the never-ending stream of emails, meetings, and PowerPoint documents. Tired of trying to make people happy, to motivate employees and achieve results. And perhaps most of all, tired of suppressing the nagging question … Is this really what I wanted. Sure I'm successful, but what's the meaning of it all? Is it worth all the sacrifices I make?

Is the C-Suite staffed by tired and dispirited executives? Is there another way? You bet there is.

NOTES

1 Charles Reich, *Opposing the System*, Crown Publishing, New York, 1995.
2 Everett M Rogers, *Diffusion of Innovations* (5th ed.), Free Press, New York, 2003.
3 Geoffery Moore, *Crossing the Chasm*, HarperCollins, New York, 1991.
4 John Hagel, *Scaling Edges: How to Radically Transform Your Organization*, Idea Bite Press, 2014.
5 Anthony Alston, Patrick Beautement, and Lorraine Dodd, Implementing Edge Organizations: Exploiting Complexity, *Paper for the 10th International Command and Control Research & Technology Symposium*, McLean, Virginia, June 2005.
6 Paul Strebel, *The Change Pact: Building Commitment to Ongoing Change*, Pitman Publishing, London, 1998.
7 Frederic Laloux, *Reinventing Organizations: A Guide to Creating Organizations Inspired by the Next Stage of Human Consciousness*, Nelson Parker, Mills, MA, 2014.

CHAPTER SEVENTEEN

Being curious – further reading

This book has been a journey for me, and I hope it has been a journey for you too. Blah, blah, blah. But I actually mean it. I have learned so much, traveled to places I'd never been, and had thoughts I'd never had before. Such was my hubris (arrogant pride inviting downfall – a sin most researchers accuse the C-Suite of) that I thought I knew pretty much everything I needed to in my field. My wife has a mental model which says: "Imagine that everything you know fits in a circle. Then what you don't know is on the perimeter of the circle. As the circle (everything you know) grows bigger, so the perimeter grows bigger." The more you know, the less you know. To know everything is to know nothing. I'm sure that's a famous quote somewhere, but I only just thought of it. I know very little, and I'm always searching for challenging thoughts, concepts that change my worldview, and ways in which I can help executives (that's my personal mission) think better and do better.

I believe that the future of the world lies in business. Governments are circling the drain, and private individuals have no power. Business can change the world for the better, but it depends on the people with power in business. I'm not asking them to give up their power, but I am asking you to ease your burden of power, simplify your life, and help us all by considering the concepts that I have laid out in this book. Just think about them. What you do with your knowledge then depends on your wisdom and ethics, and I have no say in that. But here's a list of the things that have influenced me, changed my mind, given me pause, and opened my world. It's called being inquisitive.

Chapter 1: What is management and how did it get to where it is today?

In keeping with the revolution thinking of this chapter, you should look at Corporate Rebels at: www.corporate-rebels.com. They have a weekly newsletter that I find a must-read. Articles on their website include "Cut the Crap: The Made-Up Nonsense about Generations at Work," which comments that people use generational differences to support their own prejudices. Instead, Corporate Rebels suggests that you look for the similarities and, above all, ask people what they want without making generational assumptions. Also, "Leaders: Give up Your Status Symbols and Destroy the Ivory Tower," which examines the separation of thinking (by the "top" of the pyramid) and doing (by the "bottom" of the pyramid) and the fact that the people with the most decision-making power are often the farthest away from the actual work. And, "Bursting the Bubble: Teal ain't Real," which warns against dogmatically following the "teal way," outlined in Frederick Laloux's book "Reinventing Organizations." Make no bones about it, Joost and Pim of Corporate Rebels are agitators for a new way of work and organization but are pragmatic about it.

Charles Handy's books are all a great read. He is gentle and eloquent and has the knack of saying revolutionary things without alarming you, you just become deeply thoughtful. If you're looking for a series of essays, which is a compilation of some of his best thinking, then "The Second Curve: Thoughts on Reinventing Society,"[1] is where to start.

Part 1
Chapter 2: The educational system product and its inputs to organizations

A game-changer for me was watching Sir Ken Robinson's TED talk on "Changing Education Paradigms,"[2] which really made me think, and worry, about our educational system. But he's done a lot other of talks on education – just go to YouTube and do a search on his name.

I have found the Mediun.com website a constant source of information (www.medium.com), but the Medium "Gentle Revolution" site is the one that suits my worldview best: https://medium.com/the-gentle-revolution

Charles Handy, mentioned above, also provides enlightening thoughts and insight into education. In one of his books (I can't remember which – I read it in the 1990s), he describes a vision for a school where scholars visit teachers for a half-day session on a particular subject. Thus, they get a substantial chunk of immersive learning.

Chapter 3: The generation challenge for the C-Suite

I dislike generalizations, having preached in the previous chapter that we are all individuals and should be treated and educated as such. Chapter 3 is one generalization after the next. I apologize. My aim here was to address a possible C-Suite mindset of: "Everybody thinks and does as we do." They don't. I hope the chapter provoked some thought about diversity and different thinking and working styles. I wouldn't rush to do any further reading on generations.

Chapter 4: Information inputs as a challenge to the C-Suite

As I've been involved with IT for over 40 years, I didn't need to research much for this chapter.

However, I found the book by Nicholas Carr "The Glass Cage: How Our Computers are Changing Us"[3] informative. He examines the impact of the internet, GPS systems, Google, and other technologies on our psyche, ability to think, creativity, and so on. His final chapter is a bit bleak. He concludes that it's not the technology that's at fault; instead, it's the way we use it. And that depends on our wisdom and willingness to take the hard way, even when a computer will ease the path. People being people, I don't hold much hope for a change in the way we've behaved for centuries.

If you are suffering from information overload, you might like to read the *Forbes Magazine* article "10 Steps to Overcoming Information Overload."[4]

Chapter 5: Digital everything and its effects on the organization

Again, as in Chapter 4, because much of my work has been in technology (I'm a part-time analyst for an IT research company), I didn't have to research much for "digitization as we know it, Jim." If you are interested in the digital world, I recommend that you subscribe to an IT research company. They're expensive and there's a fair amount of hype and technical detail because they cater to techies. Your best bet is to read the section in

Chapter 13 on digital fluency. The important thing is that you don't need to become a digital expert, merely fluent with the digital concepts that affect your business.

Chapter 6: The world of work

Charles Handy has done a lot of thinking on how people should work. His concept of "the empty donut" changed my thinking about how jobs should be structured – certainly my job is an empty donut. The idea first appeared in his book "The Empty Raincoat,"[5] where he talks about a job being like … an empty donut. These are ring donuts he's talking about, and the 30% at the center is filled and the 70% ring is empty. The idea is that you prescribe only 30% of people's work and let them decide what they want to fill the 70% with. This is, of course, a precursor to self-management, where 10% of the donut is "what needs to be done (the mission is the boss)," and the 90% "how" it should be done is left up to the individual.

There are many papers produced by corporates and consultancy companies on the world of work which are freely available. I found the IWG Global Workspace Survey[6] particularly enlightening, and again the Frederic Laloux book on "Reinventing Organizations" offers some insights on dealing with the "whole person" at work. There are several companies that encourage people to bring their dogs to work, for instance. Meetings are held with a bevy of dogs asleep under the conference table. I can't see how this would affect productivity adversely, and these companies say that interpersonal relationships are enhanced, as much as conflicts are reduced.

John Hagel has an excellent presentation he gave at the Singularity University on the Future of Work.[7] In his talk, he says that the dominant emotion when talking about our current trajectory in work is fear, because, currently, jobs are tightly specified, standardized, and integrated to remove any delays. The fear is because automation is tightly specified, standardized, and integrated, so the way our jobs are designed sets them up to be replaced by technology. Hagel observes that many commentators predict that up to 50% of jobs could be replaced by automation. Hagel's prediction would be 100% if jobs continue to be structured the way they are now. And that's just the start of his talk. He goes on to question what work is and how we need to move from scalable efficiency – the current institutional mindset – to scalable learning. Scalable efficiency is a diminishing returns strategy, while scalable learning is an exponential strategy. See John Hagel's website Edge Perspectives at: https://edgeperspectives.typepad.com/edge_perspectives/

Chapter 7: Pressure, change, and speed

This chapter was prompted by John Hagel's book "Scaling at the Edges,"[8] and some of his TED talks. He has written several other books like "The Power of Pull: How Small Moves, Smartly Made, Can Set Big Things in Motion," and "Net Worth: Shaping Markets When Customers Make the Rules." In both, Hagel talks about how technology increases pressure to perform, the rate of change of business, and the speed at which business happens. I've added "instant communication," which is sort of a combination of all three. With universal access to events in the world, a global company that makes an error or shafts a customer will be known about in the USA, China, Afghanistan, Ghana, and Peru, and local representatives of that company had better be ready to answer to something that happened in (say) France. Equally, instant communication requires companies to respond to a complaint or comment within one hour, because that's the tolerance level of customers.

I found Kartik Garda's paper "The Accelerating TechnOnomic Medium (ATOM),"[9] an interesting, if strident, read. He talks about how GDP (Gross Domestic Product) is no longer an accurate measure of country growth: GDP is a smoothed historical figure, while NGDP (Nominal GDP) is a more current measure of growth as it reflects growth *now*. And given the pressure, change, and speed theme of the chapter, this makes sense to me. Also, Garda's take on the effect of technology on economies, governments, and society is a thought-provoking read.

One of Garda's observations that I particularly like is:

> Whenever an incumbent industry has a misguided belief that disruption can be prevented outright by going to the government to get

protectionist barriers erected around it, that industry merely experiences a temporary delay in the disruption, after which the reversion to the trendline is necessarily sharper.[10]

I like it because it indicates that as the Daleks of the "Doctor Who" TV series say: "Resistance is futile." And I believe that – get on board, cope with the change, or suffer the consequences.

One seminal and influential paper that you should read is Gareth Morgan's "Images of Organizations."[11]

Chapter 8: Function and process thinking hold back your organization

Andrew Spanyi[12] is outspoken against business functions. He says: "The traditional functional paradigm has done more to impede customer-focused, business performance improvement over the past two decades than almost any other factor." He is a proponent of process thinking, which I am not. In a self-managed organization, processes are decided upon by the team and not imposed and formalized by management. However, I do take Spanyi's anti-functional thinking to heart.

A seminal and influential paper that you should read is Gareth Morganns's "Images of Organization."[13] He describes eight metaphors for organizations, and as I say in Chapter 8:

> [T]wo of Morgan's categories are aligned with the machine metaphor – the organization as an instrument of domination and as a psychic prison. These are harsh metaphors, but Morgan describes them respectively as metaphors for exploitation, control, and unequal distribution of power, and for ways that organizations entrap their employees.

I didn't go through all of Morgan's metaphors, but you might find it interesting to do so.

Finally, the notion of self-organizing systems is a fascinating one, originating in the scientific discipline, and usually describing an ecosystem. But its lessons apply to organizations. A general search on self-organizing systems will plunge you into this (I think) fascinating area. When I initially proposed some self-organizing "rules" for organizations in my 2001 book "Reinventing the IT Department," I deduced these organizing rules from a computer simulation described by Craig Reynolds in his paper on self-organizing systems, called "Flocks, Herds, and Schools: A Distributed Behavioral Model."[14] Perhaps, you will find organizational principles that would be useful to you in the scientific research on self-organizing systems.

Chapter 9: What customers want yesterday

In this chapter, I bring much of the previous chapters together. I talk about generations and their buying proclivities. Because I dislike generalizations, even though this book is peppered with them, I recommend that you read through this chapter and assume that, unless your product is very age-specific, all generational requirements apply to your product.

Also, give some thought to the fact that you have potential customers, even though you don't know about them yet. They are looking at your products and comparing them with others – like, and unlike, your own, and also looking at ratings (most potential customers rely more on ratings than on advertising). Give a thought to replacements of your products. For instance, if you sell pool chemicals, your potential customers won't only be looking at alternatives to your products, they will be looking at UV light sanitizers, hydrogen peroxide, saltwater, and eco-pools, which use plants to filter water. So, here's some investigation for you to do – look at alternatives to your product and think about whether you should supply the other options as well.

If your customers are checking you out online before you know about them, think about what information you are providing them with. Many, if not most, of the commercial websites I see extol the virtues and features of their products, and that's it. But recognizing that potential customers are in comparison and rating mode, provide it to them on your website. Or doesn't your product stand up? That was rude. Of course it can.

Chapter 10: Business ecosystems change everything

Have a look at James Moore's article titled "Predators and Prey: A New Ecology of Competition."[15] He says: "Successful businesses are those that evolve rapidly and effectively." All well and good, but he goes on to discuss ecosystem thinking and evolutionary principles. He goes on to say that strategic alliances and networks are merely the building blocks of a business ecosystem.

Also, look at Marko Karhiniemi's "Creating and Sustaining Successful Business Ecosystems."[16] It's an academic paper and a fairly dense read, but he synthesizes the business ecosystem theory very well.

I think the thing to remember here is that your business is already part of an ecosystem. The issue is: Can you leverage it or not?

Part 2
Chapter 11: The body, mind, and soul of the C-Suite

Now we come to the nub of the matter. Most C-Suites are too large, too cumbersome, and too distant from the business operation to be effective. Certainly, they're mainly performing the wrong role.

Chapter 12: The role of the C-Suite

Tomas Chamorro-Premuzic observed that in top companies in the USA women make up 44% of the workforce, yet 25% are senior executives, and 6% are CEOs.[17] His book "Why Do So Many Incompetent Men Become Leaders?" is worth a read. His chapters include: "Why most leaders are inept" (mostly because they are appointed and not natural leaders), and "Confidence disguised as competence," although I think he's going for the alliteration and probably means "Arrogance disguised as competence." He looks into narcissism, charisma as a myth – being liked doesn't make you a good leader – and why women make better leaders. He also covers how to fix the leadership situation.

I thought I had originated the term "outside-in thinking" over ten years ago, but, of course, other cleverer souls got there first. However, I believe that outside-in thinking is the key to understanding customers and markets, and Paul Schoemaker has written a few articles on the subject. A useful one is "Six Ways to Think Outside-In,"[18] but a search on outside-in thinking will get you several other resources you can use.

Celeste Headlee wrote a book called "We Need to Talk: How to Have Conversations that Matter,"[19] but her TED talk[20] covers some of the material in an entertaining way. In it she describes techniques for what communication "experts" reckon is the best way to listen. They include: Look the person in the eye; nod and smile; and repeat back what they said. But as Headlee says: "There is no reason to learn to show that you're paying attention if you're ... paying attention."

If you want to try scenario planning the ToolsHero website offers a useful "how-to" guide at: www.toolshero.com/strategy/scenario-planning/

Chapter 13: The skills and attributes of the C-Suite

I recommend Ralph Stacey's book[21] on dealing with complexity. His model for complexity in management decisions has helped me when talking to executives who are not making decisions because things are too complex (when are they not?) and they are in avoidance mode. Interestingly, my grammar-checker is continually asking me to choose the synonym "complicated" instead of "complex." They're not the same thing at all, as I explain in the book.

The morals, ethics, and wisdom of the C-Suite interest me greatly, probably because I seldom see them. The profit-motive and ego drive most business decisions I see – and these decisions are often wrong, in two senses of the word. They're not wise because they are distant from the area which is affected and they're often edging on the border of being unethical. Sad really. You would do well to research these topics further.

The book "Humble Leadership"[22] is a must-read. Ed Schein and his son Peter examine leadership from a human and relationship perspective. One of their chapters, "When Hierarchy and Unintended Consequences Stifle Humble Leadership," fits well with my stance on hierarchy, and command and control. I believe that real and human leadership is unlikely when executives are appointed rather than evolve into their positions. Schein suggests that a definition of leadership as "wanting to do something new and better" is fundamentally flawed, as is wanting others to go along. Getting up and going inside on a cold day is new and better, but is it leadership? Others must want to go along because of the quality of your leadership, rather than you wanting them to commit.

Chapter 14: The evolving organization

Nanci Meadows makes an excellent presentation on her company's journey to self-managed teams, discussing the myths of self-management, the critical differences between hierarchies and self-managed companies, the primary tenets that their company adopted, and how they continue to implement incrementally. Watch her presentation at TINYpulse: www.tinypulse.com/blog/self-managed-teams-creating-innovation-from-autonomy

Morning Star tomato processors are the poster-child for self-managing organizations. Doug Kirkpatrick was in the founding management team. His TEDx talk[23] went through the starting phases when they decided on their path to self-management. It's an enlightening presentation. There are a few fractal principles that were discussed before they had even ordered equipment or built the processing plant. One axiom is "the mission is the boss," and another is "no-one may give orders to another person." I'm particularly interested in fractal principles and how they can be applied to organizations. A fractal axiom is one which, when multiplied by itself, results in deeply complex organizational behavior and control – there's no need for command and control.

Chapter 15: Evolving the C-Suite

Because they hold all the cards, the C-Suite needs to evolve, but please be quick. The first section of this chapter is "The change is internal," and I believe that, which makes it hard. The external command and control mindset needs to become an internal one – what Warren Bennis called "the management of self." Have a look at Zat Rana's article "It's Not What You Know; It's How You Think." He talks about getting stuck in "habit loops" – a necessary brain shortcut for our survival – but when our habit loops impede us rather than help us, we need to change the habit loop. C-Suite executives are bringing several outdated habit loops to the decision table – I discussed one in Chapter 13 in the digital fluency section, and it's this: "I don't know much about technology, but I do know it costs too much." This started out as a baby boomer reaction to the CIO asking for funds to run the IT of the company. Back then, executives couldn't relate to CIOs very well: They talked in jargon, they practiced an arcane craft, and they were always asking for money. But back then, technology wasn't as stable as it should be, and neither was it as critical to an organization's future. This habit loop has come with the exec all the way into the C-Suite, where decisions about the future of the company are being made. It's a digital future. It's time to change the habit of rejecting tech before it's even discussed and understood. (Little rant there, sorry.) I've referenced Zat in the next section of this chapter.

Chapter 16: The way forward – the transition of the C-Suite

Zat Rana is a modern-day philosopher who, as he puts it, is: "Playing at the intersection of science, art, and philosophy. Trying to be less wrong." His website www.designluck.com is a feast of thoughts and ideas on how to be better at what we do and how we think. You have to subscribe (for free), but once you do you get access to articles like: "The Most Important Skill You Never Learned" (solitude – not being connected all the time), and "The Bullshit Stories We Tell Ourselves" (about not letting your past hold you back), and "The Only Real Way to Acquire Wisdom" (network and investigate).

NOTES

1 Charles Handy, *The Second Curve: Thoughts on Reinventing Society*, Random House Books, New York, 2016.
2 Ken Robinson, Changing Education Paradigms, Ted Talks, 2010, www.ted.com/talks/ken_robinson_changing_education_paradigms, [Accessed August 2019].

3   Nicholas Carr, *The Glass Cage: How Our Computers are Changing Us*, W.W. Norton, New York, 2014. ISBN-10: 0393351637.

4   Laura Shin, 10 Steps to Overcoming Information Overload, *Forbes Magazine*, November 14, 2014. www.forbes.com/sites/laurash-in/2014/11/14/10-steps-to-conquering-information-overload/#66d876867b08, [Accessed June 2019].

5   Charles Handy, *The Empty Raincoat* (New ed.), Cornerstone Digital, April 30, 2011.

6   The IWG Global Workspace Survey, *IWG Jersey*, March 2019. www.iwgplc.com/global-workspace-survey-2019, [Accessed June 2019].

7   John Hagel, Future of Work, *SingularityU*, Spain Summit 2019. www.youtube.com/watch?v=uAdKRvKe5PY&t=472s, [Accessed June 2019].

8   John Hagel, *Scaling Edges: How to Radically Transform Your Organization*, Idea Bite Press, 2014.

9   Kartik Garda, The Accelerating TechnOnomic Medium (ATOM), 2016. https://atom.singularity2050.com/, [Accessed July 2019].

10 Kartik Garda, *Technological Disruption is Pervasive and Deepening*. https://atom.singularity2050.com/3-technological-disruption-is-pervasive-and-deep-ening.html, [Accessed August 2019].

11 Gareth Morgan, *Images of Organization*, Berrett-Koehler, Oakland, CA, 1998.

12 Andrew Spanyi, *Business Process Thinking*. www.1000ventures.com/business_guide/process_thinking.html, [Accessed July 2019].

13 Gareth Morgan, *Images of Organization*, (Updated ed.), SAGE, 2006.

14 Craig W Reynolds, Flocks, Herds, and Schools: A Distributed Behavioral Model, *Computer Graphics*, 21(4) (SIGGRAPH '87 Conference Proceedings), 25-34, 1987.

15 James F Moore, Predators and Prey: A New Ecology of Competition, *Harvard Business Review*, 1983.

16 Marko Karhiniemi, *Creating and Sustaining Successful Business Ecosystems*, Helsinki School of Economics, 2009. https://core.ac.uk/download/pdf/80700187.pdf, [Accessed September 2019].

17 Tomas Chamorro-Premuzic, *Why Do So Many Incompetent Men Become Leaders?: (And How to Fix It)*, Harvard Business Review Press, Brighton, MA, 2019.

18 Paul Schoemaker, *Six Ways to Think Outside-In*. www.inc.com/paul-schoemak-er/six-ways-to-think-outside-in.html, 2018, [Accessed August 2019].

19 Celeste Headlee, *We Need to Talk: How to Have Conversations That Matter*, Harper Wave, 2017.

20 Celeste Headlee, 10 Ways to have a Better Conversation, TEDx CreativeCoast, March 8, 2016. www.youtube.com/watch?v=R1vskiVDwl4, [Accessed August 2019].

21 Ralph D Stacey, *The Tools and Techniques of Leadership and Management: Meeting the Challenge of Complexity*, Routledge, London, 2012.

22 Edgar H Schein and Peter A Schein, *Humble Leadership*, Berret-Koehler, 2018.

23 Doug Kirkpatrick, *Beyond Empowerment – Are We Ready for the Self-Managed Organization?*, TEDxChico. www.youtube.com/watch?v=Ej4n3w4kMa4, 2013, [Accessed August 2019].

INDEX